THE OMNIBUS OF PSYCHEDELIC NIGHTMARES

Jason A.

Synapse Books

Copyright © 2025 Jason A.

All rights reserved

The characters and events portrayed in this book are based on news reports, medical journals, eyewitness accounts, and oral histories from the era. Names have been altered for privacy.

No part of this book may be reproduced, or stored in a retrieval system, or transmitted in any form or by any means, electronic, mechanical, photocopying, recording, or otherwise, without express written permission of the publisher.

CONTENTS

Title Page
Copyright
Introduction
DOM   1
DOI   34
DOC   48
DOB   61
DOET   74
2C-P   81
DPT   90
LSD   96
PCP   113
Epilogue   123
Acknowledgement   127

INTRODUCTION

Psychedelic experiences can range from the euphoric to the terrifying, from transcendent spiritual awakenings to deep existential despair. Much of the literature surrounding LSD and other hallucinogens focuses on their potential for personal insight, creativity, and the dissolution of ordinary boundaries of perception. But alongside the tales of mystical enlightenment, there exists another category of psychedelic experience—one marked by confusion, paranoia, overwhelming hallucinations and profound psychological unraveling. This book is a collection of such experiences, some very brief and concise and others more extensive. It is not intended to sensationalize or demonize psychedelics, nor to glorify reckless experimentation, but rather to document what happens when the human mind encounters the outermost limits of its own perception and fails to return unscathed.
Between the 1960s and 1970s, Berkeley, San Francisco, and Los Angeles became epicenters of psychedelic exploration. Some viewed LSD, mescaline, and newer synthetics like the DOx family as tools for consciousness expansion, ways to break free from rigid social and psychological conditioning. Others approached these substances with less philosophical motives, seeking escape, thrill, or transcendence without understanding the potential consequences. The result was a decade of radical self-exploration, often undertaken without guidance, preparation, or awareness of the vast range of effects that high doses could trigger.
This book compiles some of the most intense and disorienting psychedelic episodes reported during that era. Where available, sources and locations are provided, drawn from newspaper articles, police reports, emergency room records, and firsthand accounts. However, all names have been altered to protect the privacy of those involved. Many of these cases come from publicly documented incidents—arrests, medical emergencies, and

psychotic breaks that spilled into the streets of major cities. Others are drawn from the underground culture of the time, where extreme drug experiences were sometimes shared as cautionary tales or cryptic warnings.

The stories contained here are, in some ways, a counterbalance to the often-idealized narratives of the psychedelic movement. While some embraced these substances as sacraments of personal transformation, others found themselves trapped in seemingly endless loops of thought, caught in landscapes of infinite geometry, or convinced they had permanently dissolved into light, sound, or the surrounding environment. Some cases are eerie and surreal—individuals who believed they had become radio transmitters, who felt themselves fracturing into multiple versions, or who saw reality melting around them like a Salvador Dalí painting. Others are deeply unsettling—people who ran through the streets screaming that they had ceased to exist, who experienced a total loss of language, or who clung to strangers, pleading to be reminded of who they were.

One of the challenges in compiling these reports is that psychedelic experiences are notoriously difficult to document objectively. Unlike other drug overdoses, which have clear physiological symptoms, bad trips exist in the realm of pure perception, where time distorts, reality fractures, and the boundaries of self and world disintegrate. While certain patterns emerge—identity loss, paranoia, time loops, thought fragmentation—each story is unique in its unfolding. Some individuals found themselves locked into nightmarish hallucinations that lasted over 24 hours. Others emerged from their trips shaken but permanently altered, haunted by the lingering feeling that something had fundamentally changed in their perception of reality.

Another difficulty is that the line between a "bad trip" and a profound, albeit terrifying, psychedelic experience is not always clear. Many of those who suffered through these events did not consider themselves victims but rather explorers who had traveled too far into the mind's uncharted depths. Some later recounted their experiences as cautionary but meaningful, while others struggled for years with the psychological aftereffects. In rare cases, those who had suffered extreme freakouts under the influence of DOx compounds, LSD, and other powerful psychedelics never fully returned to baseline reality, their lives

permanently altered by an experience they could not integrate.
These stories serve as more than just cautionary tales. They offer a unique window into the fragile nature of consciousness itself. If a single chemical can dismantle a person's ability to recognize their own name, distinguish between reality and illusion, or trust that time is moving forward, what does that say about the stability of everyday perception? Psychedelics reveal both the mind's boundless creative potential and its susceptibility to complete disarray. They are neither inherently benevolent nor malevolent—they simply open the doors of perception, and what lies beyond those doors is unpredictable.

While much of modern psychedelic discourse is focused on therapeutic applications—particularly in the treatment of PTSD, depression, and anxiety—this book focuses on the other end of the spectrum, the moments when psychedelics push the mind beyond its limits. These experiences are just as important to acknowledge as the transformative and healing ones. They remind us that these substances are powerful, that they can disassemble a person's reality as easily as they can reveal hidden insights.

This collection includes reports of high-dose LSD experiences, as well as incidents involving lesser-known but equally powerful psychedelics like DOM, DOI, DOC, DOB, DOET, 2C-P and DPT. PCP, while more of a dissociative than a hallucinogen, is included in the trip reports as it can sometimes induce visual and auditory hallucinations. The DOx family, which emerged in underground psychedelic circles in the late 1960s, is particularly known for its extended duration and unpredictable effects, sometimes leading to experiences that last well beyond 24 hours. Many of these substances were initially synthesized by Alexander Shulgin, who meticulously documented their effects, but their real-world use often resulted in extreme and unpredictable reactions.

The stories presented in this book are organized by substance, location, and the nature of the experience. Some cases involve total loss of self, where individuals became convinced they had ceased to exist or merged with inanimate objects. Others focus on time distortions, where users found themselves looping endlessly or unable to distinguish past, present, and future. Many involve spatial hallucinations—people who believed they were trapped in infinite corridors, shifting geometric landscapes, or alternate dimensions. And some are purely bizarre, involving individuals who believed they were radio transmitters, intergalactic messengers, or part of coded mathematical systems.

Each of these experiences represents an individual encountering the absolute limits of perception. Some of them eventually returned to a sense of normalcy, while others were left permanently altered, struggling to reintegrate after their glimpse into an incomprehensible reality.

These are the stories of those who fell through the cracks, of those who took a step too far into the unknown and were not sure they would ever make it back. Whether read as historical accounts, psychological case studies, or cautionary tales, they stand as a testament to both the profound power and the terrifying unpredictability of the psychedelic experience.

DOM

We begin with DOM, probably the most well known and notorious long duration hallucinogen in the literature. DOM, known on the street as STP, is an amphetamine-based phenethylamine psychedelic known for its extreme potency, intense hallucinations, and exceptionally long duration, often lasting 14–24 hours. Ironically, STP was an acronym for 'Serenity, Tranquility and Peace'. As you will witness in the following accounts, these experiences did not quite live up to the spirit of their nickname. DOM (2,5-Dimethoxy-4-methylamphetamine) was first synthesized in 1963 by Alexander Shulgin, the renowned American chemist and psychopharmacologist. Alexander Shulgin earned his Ph.D. in Biochemistry from the University of California, Berkeley (UC Berkeley) in 1955. Shulgin received a DEA Schedule I license to synthesize and research experimental drugs in 1966; however, in 1994, after publishing PiHKAL (Phenethylamines I Have Known and Loved), the DEA raided his lab and revoked his license. The official reason given was the violation of protocol by publishing synthesis methods for Schedule I substances.

The following are specific firsthand accounts of DOM freakouts, mainly from California and New York. Most of them occurred between 1967 and the early 1970s. The accounts come from news reports, medical journals, police reports, firsthand trip reports and oral histories from the era. Some users found themselves trapped in hallucinations lasting 24 hours or more, unable to distinguish reality from delusion. These bizarre stories reveal paranoia, time loops, and overwhelming sensory distortions they couldn't escape.

As if all this wasn't enough for the poor victim, the very medications meant to bring relief often made the situation even worse. Instead of calming them down, sedatives like Thorazine, hypnotics, and barbiturates frequently intensified the trip, amplifying hallucinations, paranoia, and panic. This unexpected reaction turned what was already an unbearable experience into something even more terrifying, as the victim found themselves not only trapped in a nightmarish psychedelic state but also battling the overwhelming effects of medications that their body and mind refused to accept as relief.

Thorazine, a dopamine-blocking antipsychotic, has a paradoxical reaction with psychedelics like DOM.

A 1960s-era psychedelic crisis clinic warned against using Thorazine to counteract bad LSD trips—ironically, the drug often intensified hallucinations rather than calming them.

Instead of stopping a bad trip, it can intensify hallucinations, paranoia, and panic attacks. Some research suggests that by blocking dopamine while serotonin activity remains high, Thorazine may amplify the disorienting effects of psychedelics, making an already overwhelming experience even worse.

Barbiturates and benzodiazepines are sedatives that work on the brain's GABA system to slow down activity, but their effectiveness against DOM is limited. Because DOM's stimulant effects override sedation, a user may remain hyperstimulated while experiencing dangerous respiratory suppression from the depressant. This creates the risk of erratic behavior combined with medical complications, particularly if the user becomes confused or unresponsive.

Unlike shorter-acting psychedelics like LSD, DOM can last 16 to 30 hours, meaning that any sedative administered may wear off long before the trip does. This often causes users to fall asleep briefly, only to wake up still hallucinating and in a state of extreme panic. Instead of calming them down, the temporary relief followed by continued psychedelic effects can increase their fear and confusion, making them believe they are permanently trapped in the trip.

Modern approaches to handling a DOM-like phenethylamine freakout rely more on benzodiazepines like Valium or Ativan, which reduce anxiety without worsening hallucinations. Keeping the user in a calm, controlled environment with minimal stimulation is often more effective than sedation. The failure of Thorazine, barbiturates, and hypnotics to help DOM users comes from the drug's combination of psychedelic and stimulant properties, its resistance to sedatives, and the unpredictable reactions of dopamine-blocking drugs. Instead of bringing relief, these treatments often made the trip significantly worse, leading to intensified hallucinations, increased panic, and greater medical risks.

* * *

The People's Park "Cosmic Warrior" Incident, 1967

Source: Berkeley Free Clinic Volunteer
Location: Berkeley, California

"We had a guy in People's Park who had taken too much STP. He was shirtless, barefoot, and covered in dirt like some cosmic warrior. He kept saying he could feel the energy of the earth through his feet and that he had 'dissolved into the air.'"

"Then, suddenly, he started screaming—'I don't know where my body is! Someone help me find my body!' He was grabbing at his arms, his face, convinced he had disappeared."

"He fought us when we tried to calm him down, and when the cops showed up, he ran straight into a tree at full speed. We had to take him to the free clinic and sedate him. He was out of it for 24 hours straight."

JASON A.

"The Man Who Thought He Was a Radio" – Berkeley, 1967

Source: U.C. Berkeley Student, Witness Account
Location: Berkeley, California

"We were hanging out on Telegraph when this guy—mid-20s, barefoot, hair wild like he'd been electrocuted—just sat down in the middle of the street, cross-legged, and started making static noises."
"At first, we thought he was just tripping, but then he starts tuning an imaginary dial on his chest, saying, 'Hold on, I'm trying to find the right frequency!'"
"Then he starts talking in a deep, robotic voice—'We are receiving signals from Saturn. The message is clear. We must merge into one consciousness.'"
"Cops finally came, and when they tried to move him, he screamed, 'DON'T ADJUST ME! I'LL LOSE THE SIGNAL!' They had to carry him off kicking and shrieking like a radio losing reception."
He resisted being restrained, insisting that they were cutting him off from the signal, but he was eventually transported to a hospital.
Medical staff noted that he remained in a dissociative state for hours, repeatedly asking if they could hear the broadcast and claiming to feel vibrations from the transmissions inside his body. Even after the effects of the drug began to wear off, he struggled with lingering paranoia and continued insisting that the signals had been real.

Golden Gate Park, "Summer of Love" Festival, June 21, 1967

Source: The New York Times (contemporary report, quoted in retrospective)
Location: San Francisco, California

At a free music festival in Golden Gate Park, underground

chemist Owsley Stanley distributed thousands of doses of a new psychedelic called STP (DOM). The 20 mg tablets were far stronger and longer-lasting than a typical STP dose. Profound effects can already be experienced with STP doses in the 3 - 5 mg range, so 20 mg was an absolutely whopping dose. This led to many attendees experiencing intense multi-day "bad trips." Additionally, the long onset time of STP, up to 3 hours, was unfamiliar. Many attendees, accustomed to the relatively quick onset of LSD in which strong effects could already be felt at the 45-minute mark, re-dosed, assuming that the drug was weak or inactive. Dozens of hippies reportedly ended up in emergency rooms or mental wards after hallucinating for days. A 23-year-old woman (visiting from Ontario) who took three STP pills described a terrifying ordeal: "I saw myself on fire and then I began to feel the pain of fire... If I closed my eyes I knew I would die... I was in hell," she recounted. The STP episode was short-lived, and only one death was officially linked to that batch, but by summer's end "STP" had become synonymous with a bad trip.

Haight-Ashbury Free Clinic STP Outbreak, Late June 1967

Source: Haight-Ashbury Free Clinic records (Dr. David E. Smith; summarized in Baggott 2023)
Location: San Francisco, California

In the days following the Golden Gate Park incident, the Haight-Ashbury Free Clinic received 23 STP patients in one evening and treated 32 cases over the next few days.
Patients reported panic, confusion, extreme paranoia, insomnia, and physical distress (e.g., heart palpitations, tremors).
A 19-year-old man arrived at the clinic after staying awake for 48 hours straight, unable to escape the trip.
San Francisco General Hospital also saw 13 cases of STP-induced psychosis.
Dr. David Smith reported that for every patient seen, dozens more suffered bad trips without medical intervention.

According to Dr. Smith, "At the height of the STP wave, we were getting people brought in completely psychotic."
"One young man was found sitting in the middle of the street, convinced he was a 'vibrating energy field.' He wouldn't respond to anything. He just kept repeating the words, 'There is no me. There is no time. There is no me. There is no time.'"
"It took three people to restrain him while we administered sedation."

Mass Freakout at Summer of Love Event, June 22, 1967

Source: Personal Testimony
Location: Haight-Ashbury, San Francisco, California

Hundreds of people at a gathering in Haight-Ashbury took STP unknowingly, believing it was mescaline or LSD.
STP takes up to 3 hours to fully hit, so many re-dosed, thinking it wasn't working.
When it finally kicked in, users were hit with intense hallucinations, severe time distortion, and full-body rigidity.
Dozens of people ran into the streets in terror, screaming that they were "dying" or "trapped in eternity."
Some clawed at their skin, convinced insects were burrowing inside them.
Emergency rooms were overwhelmed with people suffering from hyperthermia, extreme panic, and psychotic breaks.
One man stood in the middle of an intersection for hours, convinced he had turned into a statue.
The incident became so infamous that it made national news, solidifying STP's reputation as a notoriously dangerous psychedelic.

The Naked Prophet on Telegraph Avenue, June 1967

Source: Local Newspaper Report, Berkeley Barb
Location: Berkeley, California

"A young man, apparently under the influence of a new drug called STP, was found completely nude, standing on the hood of a parked car near Telegraph Avenue, screaming at pedestrians. 'You are all inside of my head!' he yelled."

"Attempts to remove him peacefully failed when he insisted he was 'a messenger from the stars' and that he was 'trapped in a loop of infinite time.'"

"When officers approached, he leaped off the car and sprinted down the street before collapsing in a heap near Sproul Plaza."

"He was taken to Herrick Hospital and later released."

The Climbing Freakout – "I Can See the Future", July 1967

Source: Former U.C. Berkeley Student, Oral History Interview
Location: Berkeley, California

"She was this tiny girl, couldn't have been more than 100 pounds, but she had taken a big hit of STP. I don't know how much, but it was WAY too much."

"She climbed up a telephone pole near Telegraph, yelling that she could see the future and that we were all just shadows of what was about to happen."

"The fire department came, but she wouldn't come down. She said, 'If I touch the ground, I'll disappear.'"

"When they tried to grab her, she screamed like a wild animal and almost fell. They had to put a net under her. She finally jumped, got hurt, but survived."

"Pink Wedge" STP Adulteration, November 1967

Source: Dr. David E. Smith (Haight-Ashbury Medical Clinic), quoted in Licit and Illicit Drugs (1972)
Location: San Francisco, California

A notorious bad-trip cluster occurred when a black-market LSD called "Pink Wedge" was unknowingly adulterated with STP (DOM). Users expected an 8-hour acid trip but got a 16–24 hour STP experience, triggering widespread panic. In one five-hour span, the Haight-Ashbury clinic treated 18 people for "acute toxic psychosis" – all from the same Pink Wedge batch.

Most patients were young and experienced overwhelming fear, disorientation, and the sense of "going crazy," which doctors attributed to the high dose and long duration of STP. Dr. Smith noted the strength "was more than most… had been used to," and many had taken additional doses mistakenly, since STP's onset was slow.

This incident underscored how mixing DOM into street LSD greatly increased the risk of bad trips.

The "Astral Projection Disaster", 1967

Source: Haight-Ashbury Free Clinic Report
Location: Berkeley, California

"A 19-year-old male was brought in, unable to communicate beyond the phrase 'I'm stuck outside my body.'"
"Witnesses reported that he had taken STP earlier in the day, meditated in a lotus position for hours, and then began screaming that his 'astral form had left but couldn't get back in.'"
"He became increasingly distressed, claiming he could see his own body from above but couldn't control it."
"Attempts to ground him failed. He required sedation and still exhibited paranoia for 48 hours."

The "Berkeley Police LSD Panic", 1967

Source: Berkeley Police Incident Report
Location: Berkeley, California

"Between June and August of 1967, multiple cases of hallucinogen-induced psychosis were reported to Berkeley

police. STP (DOM) was implicated in at least 30 emergency hospitalizations, many involving prolonged episodes of confusion and paranoia."
"One subject was found attempting to 'walk into a different reality' by stepping through a wall."
"Another was restrained after running through traffic, claiming he was 'inside a video game.'"
"Many subjects displayed extreme disorientation, believing hours had passed in seconds or vice versa."

The "Locked in a Painting" Freakout, 1967

Source: Personal Testimony, Psychedelic Literature
Location: Berkeley, California

"I was tripping on STP in a friend's apartment, staring at a painting. At some point, I realized I was INSIDE it."
"The whole world outside the painting disappeared. I wasn't looking at it anymore—I WAS the painting. Flat. Trapped."
"I started screaming. I thought I'd never escape. My friends thought I was joking until I tried to claw my way out of the frame."
"I don't remember how long it lasted. Just that it felt like forever."

The Never-Ending High – "Trapped for a Day"

Source: Personal Account, 1970s Underground Zine
Location: San Francisco, California

"I took STP at a party in Berkeley, expecting a fun trip. At first, everything was fine—intense visuals, colors, everything sparkled."
"Then I started feeling like I was stuck in a loop. I kept checking my watch, and it was always the same time."
"I went to the bathroom, looked in the mirror, and saw my face shifting like a melting candle."
"Hours passed. It felt like I was trapped in a never-ending dream. I

panicked, thought I'd NEVER come down."
"I called a friend, told him I was dying. He laughed and said, 'Dude, you just gotta ride it out.'"
"It lasted over 18 hours. I finally crashed and slept for a full day. I never touched STP again."

The "Telegraph Avenue Statue", 1967

Source: Local Newspaper Report, Berkeley Gazette
Location: Berkeley, California

"Police were called to Telegraph Avenue after multiple reports of a young woman standing frozen in place for over two hours, staring at the sky."
"When officers approached, she whispered, 'If I move, the universe will shatter.'"
"Attempts to communicate with her were unsuccessful. She remained unresponsive for another hour before suddenly collapsing."
"She was taken to the hospital, where it was determined she had ingested a high dose of STP."

Golden Gate Park: Multiple Bad Trips and Hospitalizations, July 4, 1967

Source: Eyewitness Testimony
Location: Golden Gate Park, San Francisco, California

A group of hippies and travelers ingested STP-laced sugar cubes at an Independence Day gathering.
As the trip stretched past 10 hours, people began experiencing profound paranoia and overwhelming sensory overload.
One man stripped naked, convinced he was "becoming light itself" and ran through a bonfire.
Another attempted to swim into the bay, thinking he could "merge with the ocean."

Several individuals became nonverbal, staring at the ground for hours, completely dissociated from reality.
One person was hospitalized after refusing water or food for over 18 hours, believing that eating would make him "cease to exist."
Multiple hospitalizations followed, and medical staff noted that standard sedation methods weren't working because the drug's duration was so long.

The "Griffith Park Time Loop" Freakout, July 1967

Source: LA Free Press, hospital reports
Location: Griffith Park, Los Angeles

In the summer of 1967, six young adults—three men and three women—gathered in Griffith Park to take what they believed was LSD. Unbeknownst to them, the substance was actually DOM (STP), a potent psychedelic with effects lasting over 18-24 hours. As the trip set in, the group began experiencing extreme time distortions and paranoia, leading them to believe they had died and were trapped in an eternal time loop.
One individual, later identified as David M., reportedly sat completely still on a park bench for over 12 hours, staring ahead and refusing to respond to his friends, believing that any movement would "reset" the loop. Another, Sandra T., started scratching numbers into the dirt, convinced she could track the passage of time if she created enough "evidence" that the moment was real.
A third member of the group, James R., attempted to "walk out of the illusion", believing that if he got far enough away from the group, he would return to reality. He was found hours later, miles away, dehydrated and disoriented, having wandered into a residential neighborhood and collapsed on a stranger's lawn. The homeowner called the police, who transported him to the hospital.
Park rangers and responding paramedics found the group in various states of confusion and distress. Some were completely

unresponsive, while others were panicking, convinced they were permanently trapped. All six were transported to a psychiatric facility for evaluation, where they were kept for observation between 24 and 72 hours.

According to hospital reports, several of them continued experiencing paranoia and dissociation for weeks after the incident. One member of the group later described the experience as "being frozen in time while my mind shattered into a million pieces".

This incident became one of the earliest high-profile cases of DOM-related freakouts in Los Angeles, as reports of bad trips and overdoses on STP were increasing nationwide at the time.

Washington Square Park Frozen in Time Incident, August 1967

Source: Village Voice, Bellevue Hospital Records
Location: Washington Square Park, New York City

In August 1967, two young men in their early twenties took what they believed to be LSD while spending the afternoon in Washington Square Park. Unbeknownst to them, they had ingested DOM, a much longer-lasting and more intense psychedelic. Within an hour, both began exhibiting extreme dissociative behavior, causing concern among passersby.

One of the men, later identified as David K., sat motionless on a bench for several hours, staring straight ahead without blinking. When approached, he refused to respond and later mumbled that he was "trapped in an infinite loop" and that every second was repeating itself. Witnesses reported that he seemed unable to comprehend the concept of time moving forward and kept repeating the same phrases over and over.

The second individual, identified as Mark J., began walking around the park and asking strangers if he was "real" or just a memory. He repeatedly asked people to touch his hand to prove he existed, but no reassurance seemed to calm him. At one point, he collapsed on the grass and refused to get up, telling those around him that "there is no future, only now, forever."

As the situation escalated, someone called emergency services. When paramedics arrived, they found both men in a deeply altered state, unable to communicate coherently. They were transported to Bellevue Hospital, where they remained in a dissociative state for more than 24 hours. Medical staff noted that both displayed extreme time dilation, paranoia, and temporary catatonia.

After they eventually came down, both men reported feeling as though they had been "stuck in the same moment for eternity" and experienced lingering anxiety for weeks.

The "Endless Time Loop" Freakout at a Berkeley Apartment, 1967

Source: Personal Trip Report, Collected by Erowid
Location: Berkeley, California

"I took what I was told was a 'nice mellow psychedelic.' It took hours to kick in, and when it did, I felt like I was being stretched out into infinity."

"The walls were breathing, my body felt like liquid, but then the trip started looping. I'd get up, sit down, see the same thing happen again. I thought I had broken time itself."

"I remember seeing my friends as demons. They were laughing, but I couldn't understand words anymore—just strange echoes. I thought I had died and was trapped in a ghost world."

"This went on for HOURS. At one point, I thought I was permanently insane."

"Eventually, I passed out and woke up 16 hours later. I swore off STP forever."

People's Park Time Warp Incident, May 1968

Source: Berkeley Barb, Hospital Reports
Location: Berkeley, California

In May 1968, a group of students from UC Berkeley gathered at People's Park to take what they believed was LSD. Instead, they had ingested DOM, which resulted in a much longer and more intense experience than they had anticipated. The effects soon turned unsettling, with many experiencing extreme time distortions and paranoia.

One student, later identified as David S., became convinced that he had been transported back to 1868. He wandered around the park asking where the horses and carriages had gone and why people were dressed in "strange, futuristic clothing." Another student, Sarah G., sat on the ground and stared at the trees, repeatedly asking if they were talking to her. She insisted that she could hear them whispering messages about the past and future.

A third participant, Paul M., stood completely still near a bench for over three hours. When friends tried to move him, he refused, stating that he had turned into a statue and that any movement would shatter his body. Parkgoers began to take notice, some even thinking it was a protest performance, until someone realized he was in serious distress and called for help.

By the time emergency responders arrived, several members of the group were showing signs of severe confusion, anxiety, and paranoia. Some had to be physically guided away from the area because they believed they were stuck in a different time period. Others reported seeing historical figures walking through the park, convinced they were witnessing moments from the past playing out in real-time.

Hospital reports later confirmed that multiple individuals from the group required sedation and psychiatric observation due to their extreme dissociation. While all eventually recovered, some reported lingering anxiety and time-related paranoia for weeks after the incident.

This event became one of the more well-documented cases of DOM-induced psychosis in Berkeley, reinforcing the growing warnings about the drug's overwhelming effects on perception and mental stability.

"The Infinite Book" – U.C. Berkeley Library, 1968

Source: Former U.C. Berkeley Librarian
Location: Berkeley, California

"There was a kid in the library, just sitting there, flipping through the same book over and over. An hour passed. Two hours. Three. I finally walked over and asked, 'Are you okay?'"
"He looked up at me, eyes wide as hell, and whispered, 'This book has no end. I turn the last page, and I'm back at the beginning.'"
"I looked. It was just a normal book. But he was convinced he was trapped in a loop. He started sobbing, saying he would 'never escape the book.'"
"We called campus security. He kept saying, 'I'm turning pages, but I'm not moving forward.' It took two officers to escort him out."

Venice Beach Sun God Incident, August 1968

Source: Venice Beach Police Report, eyewitness accounts
Location: Venice Beach, Los Angeles

On a hot summer afternoon in August 1968, beachgoers in Venice Beach witnessed a bizarre and unsettling scene. A 23-year-old man, later identified as Michael H., had taken an unknown quantity of DOM, thinking it was LSD. Within hours, he began experiencing extreme hallucinations and a profound sense of cosmic enlightenment that quickly turned into delusional mania. Eyewitnesses reported that Michael stripped completely naked and walked toward the shoreline, shouting that he was becoming the sun. As he stood on the beach, he raised his arms and stared directly into the sky for extended periods without blinking. Some witnesses said he was aggressively trying to "absorb" the sunlight into his skin, while others claimed he was reciting incomprehensible phrases about light, energy, and transcendence.

As his behavior became more erratic, he ran toward the boardwalk, where he attempted to climb onto the roof of a nearby food stand, shouting that he was about to merge with the sky. A group of bystanders tried to talk him down, but he became physically resistant. At this point, someone called the police, reporting that a man was out of control and possibly a danger to himself.

When police arrived, they found Michael in an altered and highly agitated state, still unclothed, sweating profusely, and speaking in rapid, disjointed phrases about the universe and his divine transformation. Officers restrained him and transported him to a local hospital, where he was sedated and monitored.

Medical reports indicated that Michael had no memory of the event once he regained sobriety. He later described the experience as "an overwhelming feeling of infinite expansion, followed by complete terror". He suffered from paranoia and recurring hallucinations for several months after the incident and was advised to avoid any future psychedelic use.

Individual Restrained After STP-Induced Psychosis and Paranoia, September 10, 1968

Source: Eyewitness Testimony
Location: San Francisco, California

A 23-year-old art student unknowingly took a high dose of STP, believing it was LSD.

For the first few hours, he experienced euphoria and intricate closed-eye visuals.

By hour 6, things turned dark:

He believed he was "stuck between dimensions" and "being erased from time."

Became terrified of mirrors, screaming that his reflection was "mocking him and trying to escape."

Started speaking in gibberish, convinced he was receiving alien transmissions.

After 18+ hours, his friends called an ambulance as he became completely catatonic.

When paramedics tried to transport him, he became violent, attempting to bite a medic's hand.

Required full sedation and was hospitalized for two days before he returned to baseline.

Brooklyn Rooftop Angel Delusion, October 1968

Source: Brooklyn Police Reports, New York Times
Location: Brooklyn, New York City

In October 1968, a 19-year-old man named Richard M. attended a house party in Brooklyn where various psychedelics were being used. He ingested what he believed to be LSD, but it was later determined to be DOM. Within a couple of hours, he began exhibiting erratic behavior, speaking in a mixture of religious phrases and nonsensical statements.

As the effects intensified, Richard became convinced that he was an angel sent to ascend into the sky. Witnesses at the party reported that he claimed to hear celestial voices calling him and began speaking about how he had been chosen for "the final transformation." He repeatedly told others that he no longer needed his physical body and that he would soon be able to rise above the earth.

At some point, Richard made his way onto the rooftop of the three-story apartment building. Partygoers followed, trying to reason with him, but he ignored their pleas. He stood near the edge of the roof with his arms outstretched, muttering prayers and attempting to lift his feet off the ground as if he could take flight. One witness later told police that he appeared completely disconnected from reality and unresponsive to their warnings.

Before anyone could stop him, Richard stepped off the edge, believing he could fly. He fell two stories onto a lower rooftop, suffering multiple fractures but miraculously surviving. Police and paramedics arrived shortly after, finding him conscious but still highly delusional. He continued to talk about his mission and asked when he would be allowed to try again.

Richard was rushed to the hospital, where he was sedated and treated for his injuries. He remained in a state of confusion for over 24 hours before slowly regaining awareness of reality. Medical records indicated that he suffered from lingering paranoia and derealization for months after the incident.

The case became one of the more extreme examples of DOM-related psychosis in New York City. Reports of its unusually long and intense hallucinations had already begun spreading through underground drug circles, but incidents like this one served as further warnings of the unpredictable and dangerous effects of the substance.

Subway Station Infinite Loop Freakout, April 1969

Source: MTA Incident Report, NYPD Records
Location: Manhattan, New York City

In April 1969, a woman in her mid-20s, later identified as Diane T., was found wandering aimlessly through a subway station in Lower Manhattan. Witnesses reported that she appeared lost, disoriented, and highly agitated. She repeatedly walked back and forth between platforms, stepping onto trains only to immediately step off again, as if unable to decide where to go.

Over the course of several hours, multiple commuters noticed her erratic behavior. She was seen muttering to herself and repeatedly asking strangers if the train doors were "portals leading to different versions of reality." At one point, she sat down on the floor of the station and refused to move, insisting that she was "stuck in an infinite loop" and could not find a way to escape.

An MTA worker eventually intervened after noticing that she had been in the station for over five hours without leaving. When he approached her, she became increasingly panicked, telling him that "every train is the same train" and that she was unable to tell if she was moving forward in time.

The worker called for assistance, and when NYPD officers arrived, they found Diane in a highly distressed state. She initially resisted their help, believing that they were part of the illusion. When they attempted to escort her out of the station, she began screaming that they were "resetting the timeline" and that she would be trapped there forever.

Paramedics sedated her on-site and transported her to a nearby hospital, where she remained under observation for 48 hours. It was later determined that she had taken DOM earlier that day, not realizing how long the effects would last. When she finally regained full awareness, she had little memory of the incident beyond an overwhelming sense of being "lost in time."

Medical reports indicated that she experienced lingering anxiety and episodes of derealization in the weeks that followed.

Telegraph Avenue Shapeshifter Freakout, September 1969

Source: Berkeley Police Records, Eyewitness Accounts
Location: Berkeley, California

In September 1969, a man in his early twenties, later identified as Samuel W., unknowingly took DOM at a party near Telegraph Avenue. Expecting a typical psychedelic experience, he instead found himself overwhelmed by terrifying hallucinations that distorted the faces and bodies of everyone around him.

Eyewitnesses reported that Samuel suddenly became extremely agitated, backing away from people and shouting that their faces were "melting and rearranging." He claimed he could see them shifting into different animals, their eyes changing shapes and their limbs elongating unnaturally. As his paranoia grew, he ran out of the party and into the busy street, nearly causing a traffic accident as he attempted to escape from what he believed were shapeshifting entities.

Samuel then entered a small bookstore on Telegraph Avenue, where he frantically hid in a back room. Store employees described him as sweating profusely, whispering to himself, and refusing to come out. When they approached him to see if he needed help, he screamed that they were "changing too" and curled up in a corner, covering his face.

Concerned for his safety, the bookstore staff called the police. When officers arrived, Samuel was unresponsive to their questions and appeared nearly catatonic, staring at his hands as if they were transforming in front of him. He was eventually restrained and transported to a hospital, where he remained in a dissociative state for several hours before being sedated.

Medical records indicated that Samuel suffered from extreme paranoia, visual hallucinations, and severe time distortion. Even after coming down, he reported lingering anxiety and an inability to look people in the eye for fear that their faces would start shifting again. He later admitted that the experience had left him fearful of ever taking psychedelics again.

This incident became one of the more infamous cases of a DOM-induced psychotic break in Berkeley, with police and hospital staff noting how the drug's intensity made it far more unpredictable and distressing than LSD.

Hollywood TV Possession Panic, October 1969

Source: Hollywood ER records, LAPD files
Location: Hollywood, Los Angeles

In October 1969, a woman in her late twenties, later identified as Lisa R., called emergency services from her Hollywood apartment in a state of extreme distress. She told the dispatcher that she had been "absorbed into the television" and could no longer tell the difference between the real world and the broadcast she was watching. Her voice was reportedly panicked and disoriented, and she repeatedly asked if she was "trapped inside the screen forever." When LAPD officers arrived, they found Lisa in a dissociative state, sitting motionless on the floor in front of her television. The television was still on, playing a late-night talk show, and

Lisa seemed completely unable to recognize her surroundings. She was sweating profusely, her pupils were dilated, and she mumbled fragmented sentences about being lost in an "endless feedback loop of reality."

Lisa initially refused to move, claiming that if she stood up, she might "fall deeper into the signal." When officers tried to communicate with her, she responded in a mix of nonsensical speech and television catchphrases, further alarming them. After several minutes of failed attempts to calm her, paramedics sedated her and transported her to a nearby hospital for evaluation.

Medical staff determined that Lisa had taken DOM earlier in the evening, thinking it was a mild psychedelic. The extended effects of the drug, combined with overstimulation from watching television, had triggered a full-blown psychotic episode. She was kept under observation for 24 hours before being released.

Though she eventually recovered, Lisa later reported lingering anxiety and episodes of derealization for months after the incident. She described her experience as "a terrifying sensation of being permanently recorded and broadcast to the world," which left her unable to watch television comfortably for a long time.

Topanga Canyon Temporal Breakdown, April 1970

Source: Local news reports, hospital admission records
Location: Topanga Canyon, Los Angeles

In April 1970, a group of four friends gathered at a secluded cabin in Topanga Canyon for what they thought would be a casual psychedelic experience. They had taken what they believed to be LSD, but it was later determined to be DOM. As the effects set in, the group began experiencing extreme time distortions and a growing sense of paranoia.

One of them, a 22-year-old man named Greg P., became convinced that they had been in the cabin for years and that time had stopped moving. He repeatedly asked his friends if they had "always been here" and insisted that they would never be able to leave. Another friend, Rachel S., became so overwhelmed by the sensation of being trapped in an endless moment that she started carving messages into a nearby tree to prove that time was still passing. She later said she was trying to "leave a record for my future self in case I ever escaped."

The most severe reaction came from a third member of the group, Dan L., who began hyperventilating and crying uncontrollably. He said he could "see every second stretching out forever" and that he was "falling through an endless loop of now." His distress escalated to the point where he ran outside into the woods, trying to "break free from the cycle." His friends spent over an hour searching for him before finding him sitting against a tree, staring blankly ahead and unable to respond.

A neighbor overheard the group's erratic behavior and called for help. By the time authorities arrived, two of the individuals were nearly catatonic, while the other two were still trapped in intense states of fear and confusion. All four were taken to a nearby hospital, where they were monitored until the effects wore off.

Medical staff noted that the prolonged nature of DOM's effects had intensified their sense of panic and disorientation, making them believe they were stuck in a permanent time loop. Though they eventually recovered, some members of the group reported lingering anxiety and depersonalization episodes for months after the experience.

This incident was one of several reported in the Topanga Canyon area, where the counterculture movement had created a thriving psychedelic scene. However, the rise of unpredictable substances like DOM led to an increase in terrifying and overwhelming trips that left lasting psychological scars on many users.

Times Square Neon Terror Incident, June 1970

Source: New York Post, Emergency Room Reports
Location: Manhattan, New York City

On a summer night in June 1970, a man in his late twenties, later identified as Richard B., took DOM with a group of friends before wandering into Times Square. The intense visual and auditory stimulation of the flashing neon lights, massive billboards, and bustling crowds quickly overwhelmed him, triggering an extreme psychedelic reaction.

Witnesses reported that Richard suddenly froze in place in the middle of a busy sidewalk, staring at the surrounding lights with a look of absolute terror. He began shouting that he was "being absorbed into the neon" and that his body was dissolving into colors. He then attempted to run, weaving erratically through traffic as he screamed about being "trapped inside electric colors."

A group of bystanders attempted to calm him, but he was unresponsive and appeared to be experiencing full-blown hallucinations. He kept reaching out toward the billboards, convinced that they were pulling him in. At one point, he collapsed on the sidewalk and covered his eyes, repeating that he "couldn't escape the lights."

Police were called when he became physically aggressive with people trying to help him. When officers arrived, he resisted their attempts to restrain him, thrashing wildly and pleading with them to "turn off the colors." It took multiple officers to subdue him before he was transported to an emergency room for medical evaluation.

Hospital records indicated that Richard remained in a highly agitated and paranoid state for several hours. Even after being sedated, he continued to mutter about lights and feeling like his body was "melting into the skyline."

Once he finally regained coherence, he reported lingering visual distortions and an aversion to bright lights for weeks. His case became one of the more infamous DOM-related freakouts in New York City, demonstrating how the drug's extreme sensory amplification could turn an environment like Times Square into a deeply terrifying experience.

Emergency Response for Two-Day-Long STP Trip Gone Wrong,

JASON A.

March 28, 1971

Source: Eyewitness Testimony
Location: San Francisco, California

A 29-year-old musician took STP, not realizing how long it would last. At hour 12, he became convinced he was permanently stuck in a time loop. He locked himself in his apartment, dismantled all the clocks, and covered the windows with blankets. When a friend checked on him, he was sitting in the bathtub, fully clothed, repeating "I have no beginning, I have no end."
He refused to drink water, believing his mouth was "filled with electric circuits."
After nearly 48 hours, police had to break into his apartment after neighbors heard loud chanting and banging.
He was taken to the hospital in a completely dissociated state, requiring several rounds of sedation before stabilizing.

San Diego Teen on DOM Runs into Traffic, Screaming About Aliens, June 18, 1971

Source: San Diego Union-Tribune
Location: San Diego, California

A 17-year-old boy from La Jolla took an unknown high dose of DOM with friends at a beach party. About 3 hours in, he became convinced he was being abducted by aliens and ran directly into oncoming traffic on Pacific Coast Highway. He was hit by a car but immediately got up, screaming about spaceships. Police and paramedics restrained him as he continued screaming for hours.
He was taken to Sharp Memorial Hospital, where he remained in a psychotic state for nearly 24 hours before sedatives finally calmed him.

Laurel Canyon Self-Exorcism, June 1971

Source: LAPD incident report, medical records
Location: Laurel Canyon, Los Angeles

In June 1971, a man in his mid-twenties, later identified as Mark D., attended a house party in Laurel Canyon where various psychedelics were being used. He unknowingly ingested DOM, believing it was standard LSD. As the night progressed, his hallucinations became increasingly dark and intense, leading him to believe that he had been possessed by demons.

Witnesses at the party reported that Mark began mumbling incoherently and pacing back and forth, gripping his head as if in pain. At one point, he fell to his knees and started whispering what sounded like prayers, before suddenly shouting that something "evil" had entered his body. His paranoia escalated, and he told those around him that he needed to "purge the demons" before they took over completely.

Mark locked himself in the bathroom, and after several minutes, partygoers heard loud noises and what sounded like crying mixed with guttural screams. When they finally broke the door down, they found him sitting on the floor, shirtless and drenched in sweat, holding a pocketknife. He had made multiple small cuts on his arms and chest in what he later described as an attempt to "let the darkness out." His hands were shaking, and he was muttering about needing to "cut deeper to reach the source."

Friends restrained him and immediately called for medical assistance. When paramedics arrived, Mark was in a highly agitated state, alternating between sobbing and laughing hysterically. He had to be sedated before he could be safely transported to the hospital.

Medical records indicate that Mark remained under psychiatric observation for several weeks due to ongoing delusions and paranoia. Though he eventually stabilized, he continued to experience lingering anxiety and occasional visual distortions long after the incident. He later admitted that he had struggled with feelings of detachment from reality for months and avoided any further drug use.

JASON A.

Tilden Park Cosmic Horror Experience, July 1971

Source: Berkeley Emergency Services, Park Ranger Reports
Location: Berkeley, California

In July 1971, a group of four friends took DOM before embarking on a night hike in Tilden Park, expecting a peaceful and introspective experience. Instead, the drug's long duration and intensity led to a terrifying psychological ordeal that left them disoriented, panicked, and convinced they had lost touch with reality.
As the effects took hold, one member of the group, later identified as Robert M., became convinced that he had "merged with the universe" and was no longer human. He repeatedly told his friends that his body had dissolved and that he was now just "a floating thought in the void." He sat down on the ground and refused to move, staring into the sky with an expression of complete detachment.
Another member of the group, Meredith S., became overwhelmed by paranoia and started running aimlessly through the woods, convinced that shadowy figures were stalking them. She kept insisting that she could "see them moving between the trees" and that they were "waiting to take us away." Her fear soon spread to the others, and the group collectively panicked, unable to distinguish hallucination from reality.
At one point, they lost all sense of direction and became convinced they had entered another dimension where time no longer existed. One of them, Eddie T., reportedly tried to leave "breadcrumbs" of leaves and sticks to track their movement, but moments later, he became hysterical when he saw the same pile of leaves again, believing they were walking in circles through an endless loop.
Park rangers discovered the group huddled in a ravine several hours later. All four were in a state of extreme distress, unable to respond coherently to questions. Meredith continued mumbling

about the "shadow beings," while Robert remained frozen in place, still convinced he had transcended his physical form. The group was escorted back to safety and transported to a nearby hospital for medical evaluation.

Hospital staff reported that all four experienced severe depersonalization and dissociation, with lingering anxiety lasting for days. Some reported occasional flashbacks of the experience for weeks afterward.

Harlem Apartment Identity Crisis, September 1971

Source: Harlem ER Reports, Witness Statements
Location: Harlem, New York City

In September 1971, a 30-year-old woman named Lori M. took DOM at her apartment in Harlem, expecting a typical psychedelic experience. However, as the drug's effects intensified, she began experiencing a profound and terrifying identity crisis. She became convinced that she had never existed as an individual and that she was merely a thought in someone else's mind.

Her roommate, who had not taken the drug, later reported that Lori spent hours pacing the apartment, repeatedly asking if she was real. She stared into a mirror, growing increasingly panicked when she failed to recognize her own face. At one point, she began crying, saying that she had "no history" and that she "wasn't sure she had ever been born."

As the crisis deepened, Lori became desperate for reassurance. She called multiple friends, demanding that they confirm her name and tell her about past events in her life. When they tried to calm her, she accused them of being part of an elaborate trick, insisting that they were only pretending to know her.

The situation escalated when Lori ran out of the apartment and began knocking on neighbors' doors, pleading with them to tell her who she was. When a neighbor attempted to comfort her, she screamed that she was "disappearing" and collapsed in distress. The neighbor immediately called 911.

When emergency responders arrived, Lori was in a severe state of dissociation, unable to answer basic questions about herself. She was transported to the hospital, where she remained under psychiatric observation for several days. Doctors noted that even after the drug had worn off, she continued to experience lingering confusion and emotional distress.

In the weeks that followed, Lori struggled with anxiety and derealization, fearing that she might slip back into the state of self-doubt and existential terror. She later described the experience as "being erased from existence while still being conscious of it."

The "Eternal Death" Bad Trip, 1972

Source: Underground Psychedelic Zine, Personal Account
Location: Berkeley, California

"I took STP with a few friends in a house in the Berkeley Hills. At first, it was normal—trails, colors, the usual stuff. Then it got dark. REALLY dark."

"I closed my eyes and saw myself dying. Over and over. A thousand ways. Each one more real than the last."

"I opened my eyes, but the room was wrong. It was like looking at life from the other side of death. Everything was frozen, like I had already died and this was just a memory replaying."

"My friends tried to help, but their faces melted when they talked. I was convinced I had died, and this was purgatory."

"That feeling lasted at least 12 hours. Maybe longer. I wouldn't wish it on anyone."

The Library Whispering Voices Episode, March 1973

Source: Berkeley Public Library Staff, Medical Reports
Location: Berkeley, California

In March 1973, a woman in her late twenties, later identified as

Cynthia L., took DOM before visiting the Berkeley Public Library, expecting a stimulating and immersive intellectual experience. However, as the drug's effects intensified, she became increasingly paranoid and convinced that the books around her were whispering hidden messages directly to her.

Library staff first noticed her odd behavior when she began moving from shelf to shelf, running her fingers over book spines and tilting her head as if trying to hear something. She was heard muttering phrases like "they know" and "the words are alive." At one point, she pulled a random book off the shelf, flipped through its pages frantically, and then dropped it on the floor, whispering that it was "keeping secrets."

Her paranoia escalated when she sat down at a table and began frantically writing on scraps of paper, attempting to decode what she believed were hidden messages within the books. Witnesses said she repeatedly looked around the room suspiciously, as if fearing that someone was watching her. When a librarian approached to ask if she needed help, she suddenly stood up and shouted, "They're lying to us!" before running toward the exit.

Before she could leave, she stopped in the middle of the library and stared at the bookshelves, visibly shaking. She then began yelling accusations at the books, claiming they were "hiding the truth" and that she was trapped in a coded message that she couldn't escape. Library staff immediately called for medical assistance as she became increasingly distressed and incoherent.

When paramedics arrived, Cynthia resisted their attempts to calm her, insisting that the books were "changing their words" and that she had to solve the puzzle before she disappeared. She was eventually restrained and transported to a hospital, where she was sedated and monitored for several hours.

Medical records indicated that she suffered from extreme auditory hallucinations, paranoia, and dissociation, common symptoms of high-dose DOM experiences. Even after the drug had worn off, she reported lingering anxiety and distrust of written text, stating that reading felt "unnervingly alive" for weeks afterward.

JASON A.

DOM Horror: San Diego Woman Thinks She's Been Dead for 1,000 Years, September 9, 1976

Source: Los Angeles Times (San Diego Bureau)
Location: San Diego, California

A 24-year-old woman at a music festival in Balboa Park took 10 mg of DOM, believing it was LSD. After the slow onset, she suddenly collapsed, screaming she had died and been trapped in the afterlife for 1,000 years. Witnesses said she lay in the grass, crying and unable to recognize people for over 12 hours. When police arrived, she clawed at them, begging to be "sent back to the real world."
She was transported to UC San Diego Medical Center, where doctors sedated her and monitored her for 48 hours.

DOM-Induced Psychosis: Man Thinks His Skin Is Melting Off, November 20, 1985

Source: San Diego Evening Tribune
Location: San Diego, California

A 34-year-old man at a party in Ocean Beach took a high dose of DOM, expecting an LSD-like trip. As the drug peaked, he suddenly began screaming that his skin was melting off his body.
He clawed at his face and arms, leaving deep scratches and bleeding wounds. Paramedics had to physically restrain him to prevent further self-injury.
He was transported to UC San Diego Medical Center, where he remained in a psychotic state for 36 hours before stabilizing.

※ ※ ※

Common Themes Across DOM Freakouts

DOM'S reputation for extreme intensity quickly became notorious among the psychedelic community. Its nickname is STP, meaning Serenity, Tranquility, and Peace, though high doses often produce the opposite effect. Due to its powerful mental, visual, and physical effects, bad trips on DOM can be particularly distressing and prolonged. Below are some of the most commonly reported themes in DOM freakouts.

Time Distortion and a Sense of Eternal Tripping

- Many users report a complete breakdown of time perception, feeling as if they have been tripping forever.
- Some believe that they are permanently stuck in the psychedelic state and will never return to normal.
- Attempts to gauge the passage of time, such as checking clocks or asking others, often increase paranoia and confusion.

Overpowering Visual and Spatial Hallucinations

- DOM can produce highly detailed geometric hallucinations that can feel all-consuming.
- Many users experience warping of their surroundings, with objects appearing to stretch, morph, or dissolve into intricate fractals.
- At high doses, reality itself can appear to break apart, leading to panic and a complete loss of spatial awareness.

Extreme Paranoia and Delusions of Persecution

- Some users become convinced that they are being hunted, spied on, or controlled by unseen forces.
- Paranoia may manifest as fear of government surveillance, alien abduction, or an elaborate conspiracy involving friends and strangers.
- Individuals experiencing delusions may become aggressive or uncooperative with those trying to help them.

Overwhelming Mental and Emotional Intensity

- Unlike some psychedelics that promote euphoria or introspection, DOM at high doses can be emotionally overwhelming, leading to deep fear, despair, or existential dread.
- Some users report feeling as if they have lost control over their own thoughts, trapped in an endless flood of ideas they cannot process.
- Mental loops can be particularly intense, with users repeating the same thoughts or phrases over and over, unable to escape.

Physical Overstimulation and Restlessness

- As a potent amphetamine, DOM causes significant physical stimulation, making it difficult to relax or remain still.
- Some users report a feeling of internal pressure or tension that contributes to anxiety.
- In extreme cases, overstimulation leads to compulsive pacing, erratic movements, or uncontrollable shaking.

Dissociation and Fear of Identity Loss

- Some individuals lose all sense of who they are, where they are, or why they are tripping.
- At high doses, users may feel as though they have become someone else, merged with their surroundings, or lost their mind completely.
- Feelings of depersonalization and detachment from reality can persist long after the peak of the trip.

Resistance to Help and Intervention

- Many users experiencing a bad trip on DOM become distrustful of those around them, including friends, medical professionals, and law enforcement.
- Some believe that accepting help will trap them in their altered

state permanently.
- In extreme cases, users may flee, hide, or engage in dangerous behavior due to their distorted perception of reality.

Final Thoughts:

DOM freakouts are among the most intense and difficult psychedelic experiences due to the combination of extreme time distortion, powerful hallucinations, mental loops, and physical overstimulation. The long duration of the experience makes it especially hard to escape a negative mindset, and once a trip turns bad, it can feel endless and inescapable. Compared to shorter psychedelics, DOM is unforgiving, often leaving users mentally and physically exhausted for hours after the effects finally subside.

DOI

DOI, or 2,5-Dimethoxy-4-Iodoamphetamine, is a phenethlyamine psychedelic amphetamine first synthesized in 1967 by Alexander Shulgin. As a member of the DOx family, DOI is a potent serotonin 5-HT2A receptor agonist, producing intensely vivid and geometric visuals, rapid kaleidoscopic fractals, and significant time dilation. Its effects can last between 12 to 20 hours, with some reports exceeding 24 hours in higher doses. Compared to LSD, DOI is more mechanical, stimulating, and overwhelming, often causing thought loops and difficulty in structured thinking. It also exhibits strong vasoconstrictive properties, making it an area of interest in pharmacological research on serotonin pathways. Due to its long duration and high intensity, DOI is less commonly used recreationally than other psychedelics but remains significant in psychedelic studies and neuroplasticity research.

*   *   *

The Telegraph Avenue Glass Prison Incident, November 1968

Source: Berkeley Police Reports, Eyewitness Accounts
Location: Berkeley, California

In November 1968, a man in his mid-twenties took DOI while walking down Telegraph Avenue, expecting a psychedelic but manageable experience. However, as the drug's effects intensified, he became overwhelmed by an extreme visual hallucination in which he believed he was trapped inside an invisible glass box.
According to eyewitnesses, he began frantically feeling the air in front of him, as if searching for an exit, and repeatedly banged on what he believed were glass walls. He screamed for help, pleading

with strangers to "break the walls" and free him. Despite having full physical mobility, he was unable to process that he could simply walk away. His movements became increasingly erratic, and at one point, he curled up on the sidewalk, muttering about being "stuck in a reflection."

Bystanders initially thought he was performing some kind of street theater, but as his distress became more intense, someone contacted the police. When officers arrived, they found him pacing in small circles, visibly panicked and completely unresponsive to attempts at verbal reassurance. They attempted to guide him away from the scene, but he resisted, convinced that moving would shatter his body like glass.

Eventually, police and paramedics managed to restrain him and transport him to a nearby hospital, where he remained disoriented for several hours. Medical reports stated that even after being sedated, he continued talking about "the invisible walls" and was unable to recognize that he was no longer trapped. It took nearly 24 hours for him to fully recover from the episode.

This incident became one of the earliest recorded DOI freakouts in Berkeley, reinforcing concerns that the drug's intense visual distortions and mental confusion could lead to extreme and dangerous delusions.

The Hollywood Boulevard Infinite Loop Incident, October 1969

Source: LAPD Reports, Emergency Room Records
Location: Los Angeles, California

In October 1969, a man in his late twenties took DOI while walking along Hollywood Boulevard, expecting a euphoric and visually engaging experience. As the effects intensified, he began experiencing extreme time distortions, leading him to believe he was trapped in an endless loop.

Witnesses reported that he repeatedly walked the same block for hours, stopping strangers to ask if the world had already ended. He fixated on the movement of cars and people around him,

convinced that he was watching the same events repeat over and over. At one point, he stood at a crosswalk for nearly an hour, too afraid to step forward, convinced that doing so would cause time to reset again.
As his paranoia escalated, he dropped to his knees in the middle of the street and began hyperventilating. He clutched his head and screamed that time had frozen and that he would be stuck in the same moment forever. Nearby pedestrians attempted to calm him, but he was unresponsive and continued muttering about reality breaking apart.
Police arrived and found him in a highly distressed state, shaking and staring at his hands as if they were dissolving. He initially resisted their attempts to help him, demanding to know if they were "the same officers from before." Eventually, he was restrained and transported to a hospital, where he remained disoriented for several hours.
Even after the drug had worn off, he continued experiencing lingering time distortions and reported feeling disconnected from reality for weeks.

The Sather Gate Fractal Nightmare, February 1970

Source: UC Berkeley Campus Security, Medical Reports
Location: Berkeley, California

In February 1970, a UC Berkeley student took DOI before visiting Sather Gate, expecting a profound and visually engaging psychedelic experience. However, as the drug's effects deepened, he became overwhelmed by extreme fractal distortions, leading to a terrifying sensory overload.
Witnesses reported that he stood in the middle of the walkway, staring at the arch of Sather Gate with wide eyes, repeatedly muttering that reality was folding in on itself. He claimed that he could see endless mirror images of the gate stacking on top of each other and that he was trapped inside an infinite reflection. When people tried to speak to him, he became agitated and accused them

of being repeating copies of the same person.

As the experience intensified, he began to run in circles around the plaza, attempting to escape what he described as a spiraling tunnel of time. His panic escalated when he suddenly collapsed near the gate, hyperventilating and gripping the ground as if he were afraid of falling into a void.

Campus security was called when he became unresponsive to people trying to help him. Officers found him in a dazed, dissociated state, staring at his hands and whispering about them turning into patterns of pure energy. He was unable to recognize his surroundings and had no sense of how much time had passed. He was taken to a medical facility where he remained under observation for several hours. Even after the drug had worn off, he reported lingering visual distortions and a deep fear of looking at repeating patterns or reflections, as they triggered flashbacks of the experience.

The Griffith Park Cosmic Confinement Panic, May 1971

Source: Park Ranger Reports, Medical Records
Location: Los Angeles, California

In May 1971, a woman in her mid-twenties took DOI while hiking alone in Griffith Park, hoping for a peaceful and introspective psychedelic experience. However, as the effects intensified, she became overwhelmed by extreme spatial distortions and a growing sense of existential terror.

At some point during her hike, she became convinced that she was trapped inside an invisible force field. Witnesses later reported that she was standing completely still on the trail, staring at the air in front of her with wide, fearful eyes. When another hiker tried to ask if she was okay, she began screaming that she could not move forward because she would "shatter reality" if she took another step.

Park rangers arrived after receiving reports of a distressed woman blocking a section of the trail. They found her whispering about "the walls of the universe" closing in on her and repeatedly reaching out in front of her, as if feeling for an invisible barrier. When they tried to approach her, she became more frantic, warning them that they might get "trapped too" if they got too close.

After nearly an hour of trying to convince her that she was not physically trapped, the rangers had to physically carry her off the trail as she remained frozen in place, unable to move on her own. She was transported to a nearby hospital for psychiatric evaluation.

Medical reports indicated that she remained in a state of dissociation for several hours and continued experiencing paranoia about being confined in an invisible prison even after the drug had worn off. She later described the experience as feeling like she had been placed inside a reality that was collapsing in on itself.

The Berkeley Hills Time Loop Breakdown, August 1971

Source: Park Ranger Reports, Emergency Services
Location: Berkeley, California

In August 1971, a group of hikers took DOI before embarking on a late afternoon trek through the Berkeley Hills. Expecting an introspective and visually stimulating journey, they instead found themselves caught in an overwhelming sense of déjà vu and time distortion that quickly spiraled into panic.

One hiker, later identified as Kevin M., became convinced that they were stuck in a time loop. He repeatedly retraced his steps, muttering that he had "already done this a thousand times" and that they would never be able to leave the trail. Another member of the group, Nicole T., suddenly broke down crying, insisting that they had been hiking for eternity and that they would never return to the real world.

As their anxiety grew, the group lost their sense of direction and started second-guessing whether the paths they were taking were new or the same ones they had already traveled. Michael J., another member of the group, began leaving markers along the trail, only to become hysterical when they later stumbled upon the same markers, believing they were trapped in a reality that was looping back on itself.

By nightfall, the group was in a full-blown state of panic. Park rangers discovered them after hearing distant shouting from a ravine. When approached, they were visibly disoriented, huddled together, and reluctant to move, afraid that doing so would reset time and force them to start their hike over again. Some members of the group refused to believe the rangers were real, suspecting that they were part of the loop and had already encountered them before.

Emergency responders transported them to a nearby medical facility, where they were treated for dehydration and extreme psychological distress. Even after the effects of the drug had worn off, some of them reported experiencing lingering time distortions and feelings of reality being unstable for weeks after the incident.

The Sunset Strip Neon Nightmare, July 1972

Source: Eyewitness Reports, Police Records
Location: Los Angeles, California

In July 1972, a musician in his late twenties took DOI while spending the night on the Sunset Strip. Expecting a stimulating and immersive psychedelic experience, he instead became overwhelmed by the flashing neon lights, loud sounds, and crowded atmosphere, leading to a terrifying sensory overload.

Witnesses reported that he stopped suddenly in the middle of the sidewalk, staring wide-eyed at the billboards and neon signs. He began mumbling that the colors were moving toward him, growing larger and brighter with every passing second. Moments later, he let out a loud scream and covered his eyes, shouting that the lights were alive and attacking him.

As his panic intensified, he ran into the street, narrowly avoiding traffic. He darted between cars, yelling that he had to escape the electric storm before it consumed him. Several pedestrians attempted to stop him, but he shoved them away, convinced that they were part of the illusion.

Police arrived after multiple calls about a man running through traffic and acting erratically. By the time officers reached him, he was curled up on the sidewalk, rocking back and forth and muttering about being trapped in an endless wave of colors. His breathing was shallow, and he appeared to be completely disconnected from his surroundings.

Paramedics arrived and sedated him before transporting him to the hospital. Medical reports indicated that he remained in a highly agitated state for hours, repeatedly covering his face to block out non-existent lights. Even after coming down, he described experiencing lingering visual distortions and a deep fear of bright colors for weeks.

This case became one of the more extreme DOI-related freakouts in Los Angeles, highlighting the drug's ability to amplify sensory input to overwhelming and terrifying levels.

The Sproul Plaza Identity Crisis, May 1973

Source: UC Berkeley Counseling Center, Campus Police Reports
Location: Berkeley, California

In May 1973, a philosophy student at UC Berkeley took DOI before attending a debate at Sproul Plaza. Initially, he expected a heightened intellectual and perceptual experience, but as the effects intensified, he began to experience a complete breakdown of his sense of self.

Witnesses reported that he started acting strangely during a conversation, pausing mid-sentence and looking around in confusion. He then began asking the people around him if they could confirm that he was real. As the conversation continued, he grew visibly distressed, repeatedly touching his own face and

arms while mumbling about whether he actually existed.
As his anxiety increased, he walked aimlessly through the plaza, stopping random strangers to ask them if they recognized him. When they told him they did not, he became even more disturbed, claiming that he must have "faded out of reality." He then sat down on the ground and stared at his hands, whispering that he was only a thought in someone else's mind.
A concerned bystander contacted campus security when he began crying and pleading for someone to prove that he was a real person. By the time officers arrived, he was unresponsive to questions, staring blankly ahead and muttering disconnected phrases about being trapped inside an illusion. He was escorted to the university counseling center, where he remained under psychiatric observation.
Even after the immediate effects of the drug had worn off, he struggled with lingering dissociation and anxiety. For weeks after the incident, he reported difficulty recognizing himself in mirrors and felt as though his thoughts were disconnected from his body. He later described the experience as the most terrifying moment of his life, saying that he feared he had permanently lost his identity.

The Echo Park Identity Collapse, March 1974

Source: Los Angeles Psychiatric Records, Witness Statements
Location: Los Angeles, California

In March 1974, a man in his early thirties took DOI while at Echo Park, expecting a deep and thought-provoking psychedelic experience. As the effects intensified, he began experiencing a complete breakdown of his sense of self, leading to an escalating state of confusion and panic.
Witnesses first noticed him wandering near the lake, looking increasingly disoriented. He approached multiple strangers and asked them if they knew who he was. When they told him they did not, he became visibly distressed and asked if they were certain

that he even existed.

As his paranoia grew, he started clutching his own face and staring at his hands as if they were unfamiliar. He repeated phrases about his name not being real and that he was disappearing. At one point, he kneeled near the water and began whispering to his reflection, asking if it could confirm his identity. His behavior became more erratic when he suddenly started screaming for help, begging people around him to remind him that he was real. Several witnesses tried to calm him, but he refused to listen, claiming that reality itself was rejecting him.

Police arrived after receiving multiple reports of a man in distress. They found him sitting motionless near the lake, staring blankly ahead and unresponsive to questions. He was taken to a hospital, where medical staff determined that he was experiencing an extreme dissociative episode triggered by the drug.

Even after the effects of DOI had worn off, he struggled with lingering confusion and paranoia. He later described the experience as feeling as though his entire identity had unraveled and that for hours, he genuinely believed he had never existed.

The Tilden Park Cosmic Horror Experience, July 1974

Source: Berkeley Emergency Services, Witness Statements
Location: Berkeley, California

In July 1974, a man in his early thirties took DOI alone while on a solo trip to Tilden Park. Expecting a deep, introspective experience, he instead found himself overwhelmed by an intense and terrifying hallucination that led him to believe that reality was unraveling around him.

Several hours after taking the substance, he called emergency services from a payphone near the park entrance, speaking in a panicked and incoherent manner. He repeatedly told the dispatcher that the universe was eating itself and that he was being pulled into a void beyond existence. His breathing was erratic, and he struggled to answer basic questions about his location.

Park rangers were sent to investigate and eventually found him curled up in a fetal position near a hiking trail, shaking and unresponsive. When they attempted to communicate with him, he stared past them as if he could not see them, mumbling about how everything around him had lost meaning. Witnesses who arrived at the scene said he was whispering about "impossible shapes" and "a black hole opening inside his thoughts."

When paramedics arrived, they noted that he was in a severe dissociative state, with his heart rate elevated and his muscles tense. He was taken to a hospital, where he remained largely unresponsive for several hours. Even after being sedated, he reported lingering sensations that reality was unstable and that he was still falling into an infinite void.

In the weeks that followed, he continued experiencing flashbacks and derealization, struggling to shake the feeling that what he had seen was real. He later described the trip as an encounter with something beyond human understanding, something vast and terrifying that he could never fully explain.

The Venice Beach Fractal Terror Incident, August 1975

Source: Hospital Reports, Police Dispatch Logs
Location: Los Angeles, California

In August 1975, a woman in her late twenties took DOI while spending the afternoon on Venice Beach, expecting a peaceful and visually stimulating experience. Instead, she became overwhelmed by intense fractal hallucinations that caused her to lose all sense of stability and reality.

Witnesses first noticed her standing at the shoreline, staring at the waves with an expression of shock. She began mumbling that the water was repeating itself infinitely and that she could no longer tell if time was moving forward. Moments later, she dropped to her knees and started clawing at the sand, screaming that she was being pulled into a never-ending spiral.

As her distress increased, she frantically ran up and down the beach, looking at the sky and the ocean with terror. She repeatedly told bystanders that she was stuck inside a pattern and that the world was breaking apart into an infinite series of reflections. When people tried to calm her, she recoiled in fear, convinced that they were just echoes of herself.

Police arrived after receiving reports of a woman in severe distress. When they approached her, she was curled up on the sand, covering her eyes and shaking. She resisted their attempts to communicate, only repeating that everything was happening over and over again.

Paramedics arrived and transported her to a hospital, where she remained in a dissociative state for several hours. Medical reports noted that even after coming down, she experienced lingering anxiety and visual distortions for weeks. She later described the experience as feeling trapped in an infinite loop of repeating images, unable to tell what was real.

※ ※ ※

Common Themes Across DOI Freakouts

DOI is a long-lasting and highly potent psychedelic amphetamine with effects that can last 16 to 30 hours. Its extended duration and intense mental, visual, and emotional effects make DOI bad trips particularly distressing and exhausting. Users often report a sense of being trapped in an endless loop, with no way to escape the trip once it takes a negative turn. Below are some of the most commonly reported themes in DOI freakouts.

Time Distortion and Perceived Eternity

- Many users feel as if time has stopped or is looping, making the trip feel never-ending.
- Some become convinced they will never return to normal

consciousness.
- Checking clocks or trying to measure time often increases anxiety and confusion.

Overwhelming Visual and Sensory Hallucinations

- DOI produces intense geometric and kaleidoscopic visuals that can become overwhelming.
- Some users report their surroundings morphing into grids, tunnels, or repeating patterns that seem inescapable.
- High doses can make reality appear fragmented or frozen in place, causing a feeling of detachment.

Extreme Paranoia and Delusions of Persecution

- Many users experience the fear of being watched, controlled, or manipulated by unseen forces.
- Some develop conspiracy-like thoughts, believing that people around them are not real or are part of an experiment.
- Feelings of being trapped in a simulation or alternate reality are common.

Thought Loops and Mental Overload

- High doses can lead to obsessive and repetitive thoughts that seem impossible to escape.
- Some users experience racing thoughts that spiral into panic, making it difficult to communicate or calm down.
- Certain themes, like the meaning of existence or the nature of time, can become overwhelming and lead to existential dread.

Physical Stimulation and Restlessness

- DOI's amphetamine-like effects can cause excessive energy, making it difficult to relax or sit still.
- Some users feel a need to keep moving, pacing, or engaging in

repetitive actions to cope with their anxiety.
- The combination of mental overload and physical tension can create a state of extreme discomfort.

Dissociation and Identity Loss

- Some individuals experience a complete loss of identity, forgetting who they are or why they are tripping.
- Others feel as though they have merged with their surroundings, losing their sense of self.
- In extreme cases, users may believe they have died or permanently left their original reality.

Resistance to Help and Intervention

- Many users undergoing a DOI freakout resist assistance, fearing that accepting help will trap them in their altered state.
- Some may become aggressive or uncooperative with friends, emergency responders, or medical personnel.
- Others withdraw completely, refusing to speak or engage with the outside world until the trip subsides.

Final Thoughts:

DOI freakouts are particularly challenging due to the combination of extreme time distortion, paranoia, intense hallucinations, and physical overstimulation. The long duration of the experience makes it difficult for users to find relief, and those who take high doses may feel trapped in a state of confusion and fear for an extended period. Unlike shorter-acting psychedelics, DOI provides no quick escape from a bad trip, leaving users mentally and physically exhausted even after the effects fade.

DOC

DOC, or 2,5-Dimethoxy-4-Chloroamphetamine, is a psychedelic amphetamine first synthesized in 1972 by Alexander Shulgin. As a member of the DOx family, DOC acts as a serotonin 5-HT2A receptor agonist, producing intense visual effects, euphoria, and cognitive alterations that can last between 12 and 24 hours, making it significantly longer-lasting than traditional psychedelics like LSD or psilocybin.

DOC is known for its vivid geometric visuals, enhanced color perception, and strong mental stimulation that often gives users a sense of increased focus and clarity. Unlike some other psychedelics, it has a pronounced stimulating and energetic component due to its amphetamine structure, leading to prolonged physical and mental activity. At higher doses, DOC can induce intense time dilation, thought loops, and overwhelming sensory experiences, sometimes resulting in paranoia or dissociation.

Because of its long duration, strong mental stimulation, and intense visuals, DOC is considered a more demanding psychedelic than LSD or mescaline. While some users appreciate its clarity and deep introspection, others find its extended effects and cognitive loops difficult to manage, especially at higher doses. Despite its underground popularity, DOC has remained relatively rare compared to other psychedelics, largely due to its potency, duration, and unpredictability at high doses.

❋ ❋ ❋

The People's Park Ego Death Collapse, June 1969

Source: Berkeley Barb, Hospital Reports
Location: Berkeley, California

In June 1969, a university student took DOC while spending the afternoon at People's Park. Expecting a thought-provoking and visually rich experience, he instead found himself overwhelmed by an intense existential crisis that led to a complete breakdown of his sense of identity.

Witnesses first noticed him behaving strangely when he began speaking aloud to no one in particular, questioning whether he had ever existed. As his panic increased, he started running aimlessly through the park, shouting that he was dissolving into the trees and that he had never been a real person. Some bystanders tried to calm him, but he only became more distressed, insisting that they were part of an illusion and that he was fading into nothing.

As the experience intensified, he collapsed onto the ground and began whispering that he was merging with the soil. He repeatedly ran his hands through the dirt as if he were trying to physically integrate with the earth. When paramedics arrived, they found him unresponsive to questions and staring blankly at the sky. He was transported to a hospital, where he remained in a dissociative state for several hours.

Medical staff later reported that he struggled with lingering derealization for days after the event. He described feeling as though he had truly ceased to exist for hours and that the experience had left him deeply shaken.

The Haight-Ashbury Melting Streets Incident, July 1969

Source: San Francisco Chronicle, Eyewitness Reports
Location: San Francisco, California

In July 1969, a man in his late twenties took DOC while spending time in Haight-Ashbury, expecting a psychedelic experience similar to LSD. As the drug's effects intensified, he began experiencing extreme visual distortions that completely altered his perception of the environment.

Witnesses reported that he suddenly stopped walking and stared at the ground in shock. He began shouting that the sidewalks were melting beneath him and that he was sinking into the earth. He attempted to lift his feet, but each time he put them down, he screamed in panic, convinced that he was being pulled into the street.

As his fear grew, he ran through the neighborhood, warning people that the city was dissolving. He attempted to climb a lamppost, yelling that he needed to get to higher ground before everything disappeared. When bystanders tried to calm him down, he became aggressive, pushing them away and insisting that they were also melting.

Police were called when he ran into the road, narrowly avoiding being hit by a car. Officers found him gripping the pole of a traffic light, refusing to let go. He resisted their attempts to pull him away, shouting that the streets were turning into liquid and that stepping down would cause him to drown.

He was eventually restrained and transported to a hospital, where he remained in a state of extreme paranoia for several hours. Even after the drug had worn off, he reported experiencing lingering distortions, claiming that objects still appeared to shift and move unnaturally.

The Telegraph Avenue Infinite Stairs Incident, October 1970

Source: Berkeley Police Reports, Eyewitness Accounts
Location: Berkeley, California

In October 1970, a man in his mid-twenties took DOC while walking along Telegraph Avenue, expecting a visually immersive and stimulating psychedelic experience. As the drug's effects took hold, he began experiencing extreme spatial distortions, particularly with his perception of depth and movement.

Witnesses first noticed him walking in an unusual manner, lifting his legs dramatically as if he were stepping onto invisible stairs. He moved slowly and deliberately, appearing completely unaware that the sidewalk was flat. When passersby tried to speak with him, he told them that the ground was stretching endlessly and that he was climbing an infinite staircase that he could never finish.

As time passed, he became increasingly distressed, crying as he walked in exaggerated steps and repeatedly saying that he had been climbing for hours without reaching the top. When a concerned bystander tried to guide him to sit down, he resisted, insisting that stopping would make him fall through the ground.

Police were called after multiple reports of a man behaving erratically in the middle of the street. When officers arrived, they found him exhausted and disoriented, still convinced that he was ascending an invisible structure. Even after being placed in a police car, he remained fixated on the idea that he was continuing to climb and repeatedly asked when he would reach the top.

He was transported to a hospital, where medical staff determined that he was in a severe dissociative state. Even after the effects of the drug had mostly worn off, he reported lingering distortions in his depth perception and difficulty trusting that the ground was stable. He later described the experience as being trapped in a never-ending effort to reach somewhere that did not exist.

The Golden Gate Park Tree Identity Crisis, May 1971

Source: Park Ranger Reports, Medical Records
Location: San Francisco, California

In May 1971, a woman in her early thirties took DOC while walking in Golden Gate Park, hoping for a peaceful and introspective psychedelic experience. As the drug took full effect, she began experiencing extreme dissociation and a complete loss of identity, leading her to believe that she had physically transformed into a tree.

Park visitors first noticed her standing motionless near a large tree, staring at her arms as if they were something unfamiliar. When approached, she calmly stated that she could no longer move because her roots had grown into the ground. She then raised her hands and slowly waved them, claiming that the wind was moving through her branches.

As time passed, she became increasingly unresponsive to those around her. She ignored multiple attempts from bystanders to talk to her and instead began whispering to the tree next to her, saying that she could hear it breathing. At one point, she leaned her body against the trunk and refused to let go, telling people that she was becoming part of the forest.

Park rangers were eventually called after she had remained in the same spot for more than an hour without speaking to anyone. When they arrived, she appeared dazed and was unable to answer basic questions about her name or where she lived. She repeatedly told them that she no longer needed to leave because she had found her true form.

Concerned for her safety, the rangers attempted to guide her away from the tree, but she became distressed, saying that moving would cause her branches to break. She was eventually carried out of the park and transported to a medical facility for psychiatric evaluation.

Doctors noted that she remained in a dissociative state for several hours and continued expressing confusion about whether she was human. Even after the effects of the drug wore off, she reported feeling disconnected from her body for days.

The Berkeley Campus Thought Loop Breakdown, April 1972

Source: UC Berkeley Campus Security, Medical Reports
Location: Berkeley, California

In April 1972, student at UC Berkeley took DOC before attending a protest at Sproul Plaza, expecting an experience of heightened awareness and deep thought. As the drug's effects intensified, he became trapped in a persistent and escalating thought loop that made it impossible for him to communicate normally.

Witnesses reported that he initially attempted to give a speech to a small crowd but kept restarting his sentences as if unable to complete them. As the minutes passed, his speech became more frantic, and he began repeating the same phrases over and over, unable to break the cycle. He looked increasingly frustrated, occasionally pausing to write incomprehensible notes on his arms and hands in an attempt to ground himself.

As his distress grew, he started pacing back and forth, muttering that time was repeating itself and that he was stuck inside a conversation he could not escape. Some bystanders attempted to calm him, but he ignored them, becoming more agitated and shouting that nothing he said mattered because he would just have to say it again.

Campus security intervened when he suddenly sat down on the pavement and began rocking back and forth, clutching his head and repeating the same unfinished sentence over and over. Officers attempted to communicate with him, but he remained trapped in the loop, staring blankly and responding in fragmented phrases that made little sense.

He was taken to the university medical center, where he remained in a dissociative state for several hours. Even after coming down from the drug, he reported experiencing lingering anxiety and difficulty forming complete thoughts for days. He later described the experience as being caught inside his own mind, unable to move forward in time or escape his own words.

The Market Street Infinite Reflections Panic, November 1972

Source: San Francisco Police Records, ER Reports
Location: San Francisco, California

In November 1972, a man in his late twenties took DOC while walking along Market Street. Expecting a surreal and visually enhanced experience, he instead became fixated on his own reflection, leading to an escalating panic that resulted in a public disturbance and police intervention.

Witnesses first noticed him standing completely still in front of a large storefront window, staring at his reflection with wide eyes. At first, he appeared mesmerized, but within minutes, he began speaking to himself in a frantic tone. He gestured toward the glass, telling passersby that multiple versions of himself were trapped inside and that he had to find a way to free them.

His distress increased as he pressed his hands against the window, demanding to know which reflection was real. He repeatedly turned around, looking at the people around him, then back at the glass, as if struggling to tell the difference between reflections and reality. Suddenly, he began slamming his fists against the window, shouting that he was stuck inside and needed to break out before it was too late.

Concerned bystanders called the police as he attempted to smash the glass with his bare hands. When officers arrived, he had collapsed onto the sidewalk, rocking back and forth and whispering about being duplicated. He initially resisted their attempts to restrain him, insisting that he had to escape the mirror before it swallowed him completely.

He was taken to the emergency room, where medical staff noted that he remained highly agitated and unresponsive to reassurance. Even after the drug wore off, he reported lingering feelings of detachment and an inability to trust reflections, saying that for hours, he had genuinely believed he was trapped in a world of endless copies of himself.

This case became one of the more bizarre DOC-related freakouts in San Francisco, illustrating how the drug's visual distortions and cognitive effects could create a terrifying break from reality, even in a familiar urban setting.

The Tilden Park Nature Dissolution Freakout, August 1973

Source: Berkeley Emergency Services, Park Ranger Reports
Location: Berkeley, California

In August 1973, a group of hikers took DOC before setting out on a trail in Tilden Park, hoping for an immersive and nature-enhanced psychedelic experience. As the drug's effects deepened, they began experiencing extreme visual distortions and a complete loss of separation between themselves and the environment.

One hiker became convinced that he had physically merged with the forest. Witnesses reported that he wrapped his arms around a tree and refused to let go, whispering that he could feel the tree breathing through him. When his friends attempted to move him, he insisted that he had become part of the roots and that stepping away would tear him apart.

Another hiker, overwhelmed by intense hallucinations of light patterns, ran into the woods claiming that he was transforming into pure energy. He repeatedly shouted that he was ascending and that the forest was pulling him into the sky. When his friends lost sight of him, they became frightened and started calling his name, but he did not respond.

As the hours passed, the group became disoriented, unable to distinguish hallucinations from reality. By nightfall, park rangers were called after a separate group of hikers found two members of the group sitting on the ground in a confused and unresponsive state. One of them kept asking where his body had gone, while the other muttered that he had forgotten his own name.

Rangers eventually located the missing hiker deep in the woods. He was covered in dirt, staring at the sky, and did not react when approached. When they tried to lead him back to safety, he initially resisted, claiming that he was still "becoming the wind" and that he was not ready to return.

All members of the group were transported to a medical facility, where they were treated for dehydration and psychological distress. Some continued to experience lingering confusion and feelings of detachment for days after the event. One hiker later described the experience as feeling as though reality itself had dissolved, leaving them lost in a world where nothing was separate from anything else.

The Fisherman's Wharf Dissociation Freakout, March 1976

Source: Hospital Reports, Police Dispatch Logs
Location: San Francisco, California

In March 1976, a tourist visiting San Francisco unknowingly took DOC, believing it to be a different psychedelic. While walking along Fisherman's Wharf, he began experiencing extreme dissociation and a complete loss of self-awareness, leading to a public incident that required medical intervention.

Witnesses first noticed him behaving strangely when he stopped in the middle of the sidewalk and looked around in confusion. He started approaching strangers and asking if they could remind him who he was. At first, people assumed he was joking, but as his questions became more frantic, it became clear that he was in distress.

He repeatedly asked if anyone had seen him before and demanded to know his name, growing more agitated when no one could answer. He then sat down on the pavement and began rubbing his arms and face, muttering that he could not feel himself anymore. When bystanders tried to help, he panicked, claiming that their voices were not real and that he had disappeared completely.

Police arrived after receiving multiple reports of a man acting strangely near the waterfront. When officers attempted to speak with him, he stared blankly into the distance and did not respond. He remained motionless for several minutes before suddenly collapsing onto his side, whispering that he no longer existed.

Paramedics transported him to a hospital, where he remained unresponsive for hours. Medical staff noted that he continued to experience extreme dissociation, expressing confusion about whether he was real. Even after the effects of the drug wore off, he reported lingering feelings of detachment and difficulty recognizing his own reflection.

The Boston Common Teleportation Panic, September 1977

Source: Boston Paramedic Reports, Massachusetts General

Hospital
Location: Boston, Massachusetts

A man who had ingested DOC at a gathering in Boston Common became convinced that he was involuntarily teleporting through different versions of the city. Witnesses stated that he ran back and forth along the park paths, shouting that he was being displaced between alternate dimensions. He frantically asked strangers if they were the same people he had just spoken to moments before or if they were duplicates from another timeline. As his panic increased, he stopped moving and stood motionless for long periods, muttering that if he took another step, he might end up in yet another version of Boston. His distress escalated when he collapsed onto the ground, sobbing, saying that he no longer knew if his friends were real or just variations of people he had met in another timeline.

Bystanders called for medical assistance when he began hyperventilating and clutching his head, insisting that his thoughts were folding in on themselves. Paramedics arrived and found him in an unresponsive but conscious state, unable to answer questions coherently. Due to his continued agitation and paranoia, he was sedated and transported to Massachusetts General Hospital for further evaluation.

Medical reports indicated that he remained confused for hours after admission, continuing to express fears that he was slipping between realities. Eventually, as the effects of the DOC subsided, he regained a sense of orientation, though he reportedly expressed lasting unease about whether he had ever truly returned to his original reality.

※ ※ ※

Common Themes Across DOC Freakouts

DOC's long-lasting and highly stimulating psychedelic effects can be highly disorienting to unsuspecting users, with effects lasting 12 to 24 hours. Due to its prolonged duration and intense mental and sensory effects, bad trips on DOC can be especially grueling and inescapable. Below are some of the most frequently reported themes in DOC freakouts.

Time Distortion and Endless Loops

- Users often feel like minutes stretch into hours, leading to extreme confusion and panic.
- Some become convinced that time has stopped completely, believing they will never return to normal.
- Repetitive thought loops make users feel stuck in an endless cycle, repeating the same ideas or actions for hours.

Overwhelming Visual Hallucinations

- DOC produces intense geometric patterns, color shifts, and visual distortions that can become overpowering at high doses.
- Some users lose the ability to distinguish reality from hallucinations, making it difficult to function.
- Reality can appear to break apart into fractals, shifting grids, or surreal landscapes, which can feel terrifying rather than beautiful.

Paranoia and Persecutory Delusions

- Many users feel watched, followed, or manipulated by an unknown force.
- Some become convinced that they are trapped in a simulation or under government surveillance.
- Persecutory delusions may lead users to believe that their friends, family, or strangers are conspiring against them, causing panic or aggressive behavior.

Stimulation and Physical Restlessness

- DOC's stimulant effects keep users mentally and physically alert, preventing relaxation or sleep.
- Some users describe feeling trapped in a cycle of anxiety and discomfort, unable to calm down.
- High doses may cause excessive movement, pacing, or an inability to sit still, which can make panic attacks worse.

Dissociation and Identity Loss

- Users at high doses forget who they are, where they are, or even that they exist.
- Some feel that their sense of self has completely dissolved, leading to panic.
- A few describe the experience of merging with their environment or losing all personal boundaries, which can feel either mystical or deeply frightening.

Resistance to Help and Intervention

- Due to DOC's long duration, individuals experiencing a bad trip often refuse medical assistance, fearing that help will make them permanently stuck in the experience.
- Some become physically restless or attempt to run away, believing they need to escape from something unseen.
- Emergency responders have reported that individuals on high-dose DOC can be unpredictable, combative, or completely withdrawn, making intervention difficult.

Final Thoughts:

DOC freakouts are particularly challenging and exhausting due to the combination of intense visual distortions, paranoia, time loops, and extreme stimulation. The long duration of the experience makes it difficult to escape a negative mindset, and those who take too much may find themselves mentally and physically overwhelmed for hours on end. Compared to shorter-acting psychedelics, DOC offers no quick relief once a trip turns bad, leaving users mentally drained even after the effects fade.

DOB

DOB, or 2,5-Dimethoxy-4-Bromoamphetamine, is a psychedelic amphetamine first synthesized in 1967 by Alexander Shulgin. As a member of the DOx family, DOB acts as a potent serotonin 5-HT2A receptor agonist, producing long-lasting and highly stimulating psychedelic effects.

DOB is known for its strong visual distortions, geometric patterning, and intense sensory enhancement, often described as sharper and more structured than LSD. Unlike many other psychedelics, it has a pronounced stimulating and amphetamine-like quality, leading to physical restlessness and prolonged mental engagement. Its effects can last between 16 and 30 hours, making it significantly longer-lasting than traditional psychedelics.

Common experiences include intense fractal and geometric hallucinations, time dilation, and a sense of mental clarity or thought acceleration. However, at higher doses, DOB can induce extreme paranoia, looping thoughts, and a detachment from reality. Its vasoconstrictive properties can also cause physical discomfort, including muscle tension, cold extremities, and elevated heart rate.

Because of its duration, potency, and stimulating nature, DOB is considered a more challenging psychedelic, requiring careful dosage control. While some users appreciate its sharp visuals and heightened awareness, others find its long duration and potential for mental looping overwhelming. Though it has remained less popular than LSD or psilocybin, DOB continues to be of interest in psychedelic research and underground use due to its unique combination of intense visuals and stimulant-like effects.

At high doses, DOB poses significant risks due to its powerful vasoconstrictive properties, which can severely restrict blood flow and raise blood pressure. As a stimulant, DOB increases the release of serotonin, dopamine, and norepinephrine, leading to heightened alertness and stimulation. However, at higher doses, this vasoconstriction can cause blood vessels to tighten, reducing circulation to vital organs and tissues. Users may experience symptoms such as severe chest pain, headaches, numbness in extremities, and a risk of cardiovascular events like heart attack or stroke. This dangerous side effect is particularly concerning for individuals with pre-existing health conditions, and the prolonged duration of DOB's effects further heightens the risk, as users may be exposed to these risks for many hours, sometimes up to 24 hours or more.

* * *

The People's Park Geometric Collapse, August 1969

Source: Berkeley Barb, Medical Reports
Location: Berkeley, California

In August 1969, a man in his late twenties took DOB at People's Park, expecting a psychedelic experience similar to LSD. As the drug took effect, he began experiencing extreme geometric hallucinations that became overwhelming and disorienting.
Witnesses reported that he initially appeared fascinated, staring at the ground as if mesmerized by invisible patterns. Within minutes, his fascination turned to distress as he repeatedly fell to the ground, claiming that reality was collapsing into triangular fragments. He attempted to position his body in strange angles, insisting that he needed to align himself with the shapes to avoid being absorbed into them.
As bystanders gathered to see what was happening, he became more agitated and started shouting that he was trapped inside a pattern that he could not escape. He pointed at the trees and sky, claiming that everything had transformed into a shifting series of grids and crystalline structures. He moved erratically, sometimes attempting to walk in a straight line but suddenly stopping and

falling again, as if the ground beneath him had disappeared.

Police were called after he remained frozen in place for several minutes, staring blankly ahead and refusing to respond when spoken to. Officers and paramedics found him in a catatonic state, still attempting to adjust his posture as if he were part of an abstract mathematical equation. He resisted being moved, telling them that any change in his position would break reality.

He was transported to a hospital, where he remained in a dissociative and paranoid state for hours. Even after the drug's effects began to wear off, he reported lingering visual distortions and continued to see geometric grids overlaying his vision. He later described the experience as feeling as though he had become trapped inside the structure of reality itself, unable to find a way out.

This case became one of the more widely discussed DOB freakouts in Berkeley, illustrating how the drug's intense visual distortions and cognitive effects could lead to severe confusion and an overwhelming sense of being lost in an abstract world.

The Hollywood Boulevard Geometric Paranoia, September 1969

Source: LAPD Reports, Emergency Room Records
Location: Los Angeles, California

In September 1969, a man in his late twenties took DOB while walking along Hollywood Boulevard, expecting a stimulating and visually immersive psychedelic experience. As the drug took effect, he became fixated on the geometric patterns created by the neon lights and street signs, which appeared to shift and rearrange in complex formations.

Witnesses first noticed him standing motionless in the middle of the sidewalk, tracing shapes in the air with his hands. He muttered to himself about a hidden code embedded in the lights and became increasingly agitated, insisting that he was deciphering a message meant specifically for him. When people tried to walk past, he blocked their way and demanded to know if they could see the same symbols he was seeing.

As time passed, he became paranoid, accusing random pedestrians of being part of a system designed to trap him in an endless loop of repeating shapes. His behavior escalated when he suddenly turned and ran into the street, dodging cars and yelling that he needed to escape before the patterns locked him in permanently. Drivers honked and swerved to avoid him, and multiple bystanders called the police.

When officers arrived, he was pacing in circles, looking up at the flashing billboards and repeating fragmented phrases about being trapped inside a geometric machine. He resisted when officers tried to approach him, telling them that they were part of the system and that their radios were interfering with his attempts to break free.

He was eventually restrained and transported to a hospital, where he remained highly agitated for several hours. Medical staff reported that he continued seeing shifting geometric patterns on the walls and refused to close his eyes, fearing that he would lose himself in the repeating shapes. Even after the drug began to wear off, he described lingering visual distortions and a sense of detachment from reality for several days.

The Telegraph Avenue Mechanical Time Loop, May 1971

Source: Eyewitness Accounts, Berkeley Police Reports
Location: Berkeley, California

In May 1971, a woman in her late twenties took DOB while walking on Telegraph Avenue. As the drug took hold, she began experiencing extreme distortions in her perception of time, leading to an overwhelming sense of repetition that spiraled into paranoia.

Witnesses first noticed her walking with an unusual hesitation, pausing every few steps to look around as if expecting something to change. She repeatedly checked the time on her wristwatch, growing visibly distressed each time she looked at it. As minutes passed, she began retracing her steps, walking back and forth between the same locations, convinced that she was stuck in a mechanical time loop.

She then started adjusting her posture and moving her hands in rigid, deliberate motions, as if she were trying to reset her own body. Some people attempted to ask if she needed help, but she ignored them and continued adjusting her arms and legs in a mechanical fashion, mumbling that she needed to "calibrate the sequence" before time could start again.

As her panic grew, she sat down on the pavement, gripping her head and repeating that time had malfunctioned and that she was permanently stuck. When police arrived, she was unresponsive to their questions and kept moving her hands in precise, repetitive motions as if she were manually rewinding herself.

She was eventually taken to a hospital, where she remained highly anxious for several hours, still convinced that her body was caught in a repeating cycle. Even after the effects of the drug began to wear off, she reported lingering feelings of déjà vu and continued to question whether she had escaped the loop.

This case became one of the more unsettling DOB-related incidents in Berkeley, demonstrating how the drug's distortions of time and movement could lead to a state of complete psychological entrapment.

The Griffith Park Infinite Maze Incident, June 1971

Source: Park Ranger Reports, Medical Records
Location: Los Angeles, California

In June 1971, a woman in her late twenties took DOB while hiking in Griffith Park, hoping for an introspective and visually immersive experience. As the drug's effects deepened, she became overwhelmed by severe spatial distortions, leading her to believe that she was trapped inside an infinite maze.

Hikers who encountered her reported that she appeared confused, repeatedly looking over her shoulder and hesitating before taking steps forward. She kept retracing her path, stopping every few feet to look around in frustration. When asked if she needed help, she insisted that she had already walked the same route many times but could not remember how to escape.

As her paranoia grew, she began marking the trail with sticks and rocks, convinced that something was resetting her location each time she moved forward. She became increasingly frantic, running short distances before stopping abruptly, claiming that the trees were shifting around her and creating a loop.

Park rangers were called after another group of hikers found her near a trailhead, standing completely still and staring at the ground. When approached, she refused to move, whispering that she was stuck between two dimensions and that stepping in any direction would trap her forever.

After several attempts to calm her down, rangers had to assist her off the trail. She was transported to a medical facility, where she remained anxious and disoriented for several hours. Even after the effects of the drug wore off, she continued expressing doubts about whether she had actually escaped the maze or if she was still caught inside it.

The UC Berkeley Infinite Echo Incident, October 1972

Source: UC Berkeley Campus Security, Medical Records
Location: Berkeley, California

In October 1972, a student at UC Berkeley took DOB before visiting on campus, expecting a stimulating and thought-provoking psychedelic experience. As the effects deepened, he became trapped in an overwhelming auditory hallucination that convinced him he was stuck in an infinite loop of sound.

Witnesses first noticed him clapping his hands repeatedly and tilting his head as if listening for something. At first, he seemed amused, but his expression quickly changed to one of concern. He began looking around anxiously and asked those near him if they could still hear the echoes. When no one else noticed anything unusual, he grew increasingly alarmed and started clapping louder, convinced that the sound of his hands was being played back to him endlessly.

His distress escalated as he began shouting that he was trapped in an endless wave of sound. He covered his ears and winced, claiming that every noise was bouncing back and layering on top of itself. He started running in circles, stopping every few seconds to listen as if trying to escape an invisible reverberation.

As his panic increased, he grabbed his head and screamed that his thoughts were being played back on a loop. He asked people around him if they could hear what he was thinking and accused strangers of repeating his words before he even spoke them. Some bystanders tried to reassure him, but he refused to believe that time was moving forward normally.

Campus security intervened when he collapsed onto the pavement, covering his ears and rocking back and forth. He was unresponsive to questions and continued whispering that everything was repeating and that he would never escape the echo.

He was transported to a medical facility, where he remained in a state of severe anxiety for several hours. Even after the effects of the drug had worn off, he reported experiencing occasional auditory distortions and paranoia about sounds looping back at him.

The Sunset Strip Fractal Breakdown, March 1973

Source: Eyewitness Reports, LAPD Incident Logs
Location: Los Angeles, California

In March 1973, a musician took DOB while spending the night on the Sunset Strip, expecting an experience of heightened creativity and sensory enhancement. As the effects took hold, he became overwhelmed by intense visual fractals that distorted his perception of reality, leading to a public breakdown.

Witnesses first noticed him standing on the sidewalk, staring at the headlights of passing cars with an expression of awe and terror. He muttered about the lights stretching into infinity and began reaching out as if trying to grab something that was not there. Moments later, he started moving his arms in slow, exaggerated motions, saying that space had turned into liquid geometry and that he needed to swim through it.

His behavior escalated when he suddenly turned and ran into the street, narrowly avoiding oncoming traffic. He shouted that he was dissolving into pure light and no longer part of the physical world. Pedestrians tried to calm him, but he was unresponsive, continuing to speak in fragmented sentences about time breaking apart and his body losing its form.

Police arrived after multiple reports of a man behaving erratically in traffic. By the time officers reached him, he was sitting on the ground, staring at his hands and whispering that they were turning into infinite patterns. He resisted being touched, claiming that he was already fading into the fractal and that any interference would cause him to shatter completely.

Paramedics transported him to a hospital, where he remained in a dissociative state for several hours. Even after the drug began to wear off, he continued reporting visual distortions and a fear that he was still dissolving. He later described the experience as being trapped in an infinite, shifting reality with no clear way back.

The Tilden Park Reality Fracture, June 1974

Source: Park Ranger Reports, Emergency Room Records
Location: Berkeley, California

In June 1974, a group of hikers took DOB before setting out on a trail in Tilden Park, expecting an immersive and visually enhanced experience in nature. As the drug's effects took hold, they began experiencing extreme distortions in space and perception, leading to a collective state of fear and confusion.

One hiker suddenly stopped on the trail and pointed at the sky, claiming that it had split open and that he could see into an alternate dimension. He described seeing strange, shifting colors in the sky and insisted that he was watching another version of reality bleed into their own. Another member of the group, growing increasingly anxious, started touching his arms and legs, repeatedly asking if his body was still attached. He told the others that he could feel himself separating into pieces and that he needed to hold himself together to avoid disappearing completely. As their fear grew, the group became disoriented and started running in different directions, believing they had crossed into a different timeline. Some of them attempted to retrace their steps, convinced that they had entered a broken part of reality where space was looping back on itself. Others sat down and refused to move, certain that taking another step would cause them to fall into an invisible void.

Park rangers were alerted when hikers in another group reported seeing several distressed individuals wandering aimlessly through the woods. When the rangers arrived, they found some members of the group lying on the ground, staring blankly into the trees, while others were whispering about the sky fracturing. One individual attempted to explain that they had been split into multiple versions of themselves and that they could feel their other selves existing in parallel realities.

The group was eventually escorted out of the park and transported to a hospital, where they remained in a state of confusion and paranoia for several hours. Even after the drug had worn off, some of them continued to experience lingering feelings of dissociation and reported occasional visual distortions for days.

This case became one of the more unsettling DOB-related freakouts in Berkeley, illustrating how the drug's extreme spatial and perceptual distortions could lead to a terrifying sense of reality breaking apart.

The Echo Park Language Collapse, July 1974

Source: Los Angeles Psychiatric Records, Witness Statements

JASON A.

Location: Los Angeles, California

In July 1974, a man took DOB at a gathering in Echo Park, expecting a deeply introspective and sensory-enhancing experience. As the drug took effect, he became increasingly focused on the words people were saying around him. At first, he was fascinated by the way conversations sounded, but within an hour, his fascination turned into confusion and panic.

Witnesses reported that he began staring intensely at people while they spoke, tilting his head as if trying to understand a foreign language. He eventually stopped responding in full sentences, instead repeating random words in a slow, uncertain tone. When asked if he was okay, he shook his head and said that words were losing their meaning.

As his distress increased, he grabbed a book from a table and began flipping through the pages frantically, scanning the text with wide, panicked eyes. He repeatedly asked what the words meant and why they looked different. When he was unable to process what he was reading, he dropped the book and started pulling at his hair, whispering that he was losing language and that soon he would not be able to think anymore.

His panic escalated when he began speaking nonsense syllables, as if trying to reconstruct language from memory. At one point, he started crying and ran his hands over newspapers and books, muttering that the world had lost its meaning. Witnesses called for medical assistance when he began hyperventilating and begging people to remind him how to talk.

Paramedics transported him to a hospital, where he remained unresponsive to verbal communication for several hours. Even after the effects of the drug had worn off, he continued struggling to form coherent sentences and experienced lingering paranoia about whether he would forget how to speak again.

This case became one of the more unusual DOB-related freakouts in Los Angeles, illustrating how the drug's cognitive distortions could lead to a total breakdown of language comprehension and a terrifying loss of connection to reality.

* * *

Common Themes Across DOB Freakouts

DOB's extended duration, combined with its powerful mental and physical stimulation, makes DOB one of the more challenging psychedelics when a trip goes bad. Users who take too much often report feeling trapped in an overwhelming state of altered consciousness with no way to escape. Below are some of the most commonly reported themes in DOB freakouts.

Time Distortion and the Feeling of Being Stuck

- Many users report that time feels frozen or looping, making the trip feel like an eternity.
- Some become convinced that they will never return to normal and that they are permanently altered.
- Checking clocks or attempting to measure time only increases feelings of anxiety and confusion.

Intense Visual Hallucinations and Perceptual Overload

- DOB produces highly detailed geometric and fractal hallucinations that can be overwhelming.
- Users often report seeing their surroundings shift into intricate patterns that make reality feel unstable.
- At high doses, visuals can become so intense that users feel disconnected from their environment.

Extreme Paranoia and Delusional Thinking

- Some users develop strong beliefs that they are being watched, followed, or controlled by external forces.
- Common delusions include thinking they are part of a secret

experiment or that they are being observed by government agencies or extraterrestrial beings.
- In some cases, users believe that the people around them are not real or that they themselves have ceased to exist.

Thought Loops and Mental Overload

- DOB's stimulating effects can lead to repetitive, obsessive thought patterns that are impossible to escape.
- Some users become trapped in existential loops, questioning reality, their identity, or the nature of consciousness for hours on end.
- Racing thoughts and an inability to slow down the mind can contribute to severe anxiety and panic.

Physical Overstimulation and Restlessness

- As a phenethylamine stimulant, DOB can cause physical tension, excessive energy, and an inability to sit still.
- Some users describe feeling a strong inner pressure or restlessness that prevents them from relaxing.
- In extreme cases, users experience uncontrollable shaking, muscle tension, or compulsive movement.

Dissociation and Loss of Identity

- High doses can lead to a complete detachment from self, with users forgetting who they are or what they are doing.
- Some users feel as though they have merged with their surroundings or become part of an abstract concept.
- A few report terrifying experiences of ego death where they believe they have permanently lost their sense of self.

Resistance to Help and Unpredictable Behavior

- Many users in the middle of a DOB freakout refuse assistance,

believing that seeking help will make things worse.
- Some may lash out or resist medical intervention due to fear of being trapped in an altered state forever.
- Others may become completely withdrawn, refusing to speak or move until the trip naturally subsides.

Final Thoughts:

DOB freakouts are particularly difficult due to the drug's extreme duration, intense visuals, strong mental loops, and stimulating physical effects. Unlike shorter psychedelics, DOB provides no easy escape from a bad trip, and those who take too much often feel trapped in overwhelming paranoia, confusion, and sensory overload for hours on end. Once the trip turns negative, users may experience exhaustion, anxiety, and emotional distress that lasts long after the drug itself has worn off.

DOET

DOET, or 2,5-Dimethoxy-4-ethylamphetamine, is a psychedelic amphetamine first synthesized in the 1960s by Alexander Shulgin. As a member of the DOx family, DOET acts as a serotonin 5-HT2A receptor agonist, producing long-lasting psychedelic effects that can last between 12 and 20 hours.

DOET is known for its unique blend of mental stimulation, visual distortions, and deep cognitive alterations. Unlike LSD or psilocybin, which often induce fluid and organic visuals, DOET's effects are more structured, with users frequently reporting intricate geometric patterns, time dilation, and enhanced abstract thinking. At lower doses, it can create a state of heightened awareness and euphoria, while at higher doses, it can lead to intense thought loops, paranoia, and dissociative episodes.

One of DOET's distinguishing characteristics is its impact on language and cognition. Some users have reported experiencing difficulties with speech, reading, or even understanding language, as well as a strong sense of detachment from their own identity. While some find its introspective and analytical effects useful for deep thought, others describe it as mentally overwhelming, leading to looping thoughts or confusion.

Due to its long duration, unpredictable cognitive effects, and less euphoric nature compared to other psychedelics, DOET never gained widespread popularity. However, it remains notable for its role in early psychedelic research and its unique ability to alter perception in ways distinct from LSD, mescaline, or psilocybin.

❋ ❋ ❋

The People's Park Thought Loop Collapse, June 1968

Source: Berkeley Barb, Hospital Reports

Location: Berkeley, California

In June 1968, a man took DOET while at People's Park, expecting a mentally expansive and visually stimulating experience. As the drug's effects intensified, he became trapped in an overwhelming and inescapable thought loop that spiraled into extreme distress.

Witnesses first noticed him pacing in circles, repeatedly muttering the same phrase under his breath. At first, people assumed he was deep in thought, but as time passed, he began speaking the same sentence out loud over and over again. When approached, he seemed unable to engage in normal conversation, instead restarting the same phrase as if his mind could not move forward.

As his distress grew, he grabbed his head and began pulling at his hair, insisting that his mind had become a broken record and that he could not escape the cycle. He asked those around him if time was repeating and if they were also stuck in the same moment. Some bystanders tried to reassure him that he was okay, but he became increasingly agitated, convinced that reality was replaying itself indefinitely.

At one point, he fell to his knees and stared at his hands, whispering that he was dissolving into his own thoughts. He refused to respond to attempts to distract him, growing more frantic each time he realized he was still trapped in the same mental loop.

Paramedics arrived after someone reported that he had been saying the same thing for hours without stopping. When they attempted to communicate with him, he remained unresponsive, staring blankly and repeating words in a robotic tone. He was eventually sedated and taken to a hospital, where medical staff noted that even after the drug had worn off, he was still struggling to form new thoughts and feared he would become stuck in another loop.

The Berkeley Campus Language Breakdown, May 1971

JASON A.

Source: UC Berkeley Campus Security, Medical Reports
Location: Berkeley, California

In May 1971, a student at UC Berkeley took DOET before attending a campus rally, expecting an intellectually stimulating experience. Instead, he suffered a sudden and complete breakdown in his ability to understand and process language, leading to an extreme psychological crisis.
Witnesses first noticed that he had stopped responding normally to conversation, instead staring at people with a confused expression. When someone asked him a question, he opened his mouth as if to answer but then hesitated, struggling to form words. He began shaking his head, saying that the words did not make sense anymore.
As his distress grew, he picked up a book and started flipping through the pages frantically, scanning the text as if trying to remember how to read. After a few minutes, he threw the book down and muttered that the letters were shifting and no longer forming real words. He then began repeating simple words aloud, his voice growing more panicked each time, as if testing whether they still had meaning.
His anxiety increased rapidly, and he started pulling at his hair and pacing in circles. He asked people around him why they were speaking in a language he could not understand, even though they were speaking English. He clutched his head and groaned in frustration, then began making sounds that resembled speech but had no real structure, as if trying to recreate language from memory.
Campus security was called when he collapsed near the campus entrance on Bancroft, holding his hands over his ears and shouting nonsense syllables. When officers arrived, he did not respond to questions, instead staring at their mouths as if watching for meaning that he could no longer grasp.
He was taken to a hospital, where he remained unresponsive to spoken communication for several hours. Even after the effects of the drug wore off, he continued to express fear that he had

permanently lost his ability to understand language. He later described the experience as being trapped in a world where words had stopped existing.

This case became one of the more extreme DOET-related incidents at UC Berkeley, demonstrating how the drug's cognitive distortions could lead to a complete breakdown in linguistic comprehension and an overwhelming sense of isolation.

The "Infinite Copies" Paranoia – Kenmore Square, October 31, 1976

Source: Boston Herald
Location: Boston, Massachusetts

A man in his mid-30s took a large dose of DOET and was later seen frantically pacing near Kenmore Square, muttering to himself. He ran into traffic, waving his arms wildly.
According to a taxi driver: "He ran right in front of my cab, waving his arms like he was trying to flag down something that wasn't there. When I honked, he screamed and covered his ears, like the sound was hurting him."
Witnesses reported him talking about "multiplying" and "infinite versions" of himself.
A pedestrian reported: "He was muttering something about 'multiplying' and 'infinite versions' of himself. When someone tried to calm him down, he screamed, 'Don't touch me! You'll split again!' and ran into traffic."
Police arrived, and he resisted, screaming about needing to find 'the first version of himself.'
A police officer on the scene said: "We had to restrain him because he kept trying to run in different directions like he couldn't decide which way was real. He was shouting, 'I need to find the first me before they all catch up!'"
He was taken to hospital where he was sedated and placed under psychiatric care for 72 hours.
The man later described his experience as "escaping from infinite

versions of himself."

* * *

Common Themes Across DOET Freakouts

While not as widely used as other psychedelics in the amphetamine family, DOET can produce deeply immersive hallucinations, cognitive shifts, and emotional intensity. Its combination of mental stimulation and altered perception makes bad trips particularly distressing, often leaving users feeling overwhelmed, stuck in thought loops, or disconnected from reality. Below are some of the most commonly reported themes in DOET freakouts.

Time Distortion and the Sense of a Never-Ending Trip

- Many users report that time feels stretched or frozen, leading to confusion and anxiety.
- Some become convinced that they are permanently altered or that the trip will never end.
- The feeling of being caught in an infinite moment can lead to panic and mental exhaustion.

Intense Visual and Auditory Hallucinations

- DOET produces vivid geometric patterns, light trails, and shifting colors that can become overwhelming.
- At high doses, objects appear to morph, stretch, or take on surreal qualities that make reality feel distorted.
- Some users report auditory hallucinations, such as hearing distant voices, music, or environmental sounds repeating in loops.

Paranoia and Delusions of Persecution

- Users often feel as though they are being watched or followed, leading to intense fear.
- Some develop delusions that they are trapped in a simulation or part of an experiment.
- In extreme cases, users may believe that the people around them are conspiring against them, leading to distrust and withdrawal.

Thought Loops and Cognitive Overload

- DOET is known for its ability to induce repetitive thought loops that can feel impossible to break.
- Users may become obsessed with trying to figure out reality, only to spiral further into confusion.
- Some report overwhelming existential thoughts, questioning their own identity, purpose, or whether they even exist.

Physical Stimulation and Restlessness

- DOET has stimulating properties that make it difficult to sit still or relax.
- Some users feel a sense of internal pressure, as if they are vibrating or filled with excess energy.
- In extreme cases, users engage in compulsive pacing, shaking, or other restless behaviors to cope with anxiety.

Dissociation and Loss of Self

- High doses can cause users to feel completely disconnected from their body or identity.
- Some report merging with their surroundings or feeling as though they are dissolving into an abstract state.
- In extreme cases, users believe they have permanently lost their sense of self and will never return to normal.

Resistance to Help and Confusion About Reality

- Many individuals experiencing a bad trip on DOET resist help, believing that intervention will make things worse.
- Some become agitated or uncooperative, fearing that those trying to help are part of a conspiracy.
- Others withdraw entirely, unable to speak or interact with reality until the effects wear off.

Final Thoughts:

DOET freakouts can be intensely disorienting and exhausting, often characterized by deep paranoia, sensory overload, time loops, and a sense of losing one's identity. Its long duration makes it especially challenging for those struggling with a bad trip, as feelings of anxiety and confusion can persist for hours. Unlike shorter psychedelics, DOET does not provide an easy way out of a negative state, leaving users feeling mentally and physically drained even after the effects fade.

2C-P

2C-P, or 2,5-Dimethoxy-4-propylphenethylamine, is a potent psychedelic phenethylamine first synthesized by Alexander Shulgin in the 1970s. It was documented in his book PiHKAL: A Chemical Love Story, where he described its long duration, high potency, and intense mental and visual effects.

As a member of the 2C family, 2C-P primarily acts as a serotonin 5-HT2A receptor agonist, producing powerful psychedelic experiences that can last between 10 and 20 hours, with some reports extending even longer. Compared to other 2C compounds like 2C-B or 2C-E, 2C-P is known for its delayed onset, taking up to three hours to fully manifest, which has led to accidental overdoses by users mistaking it for a weaker substance.

The effects of 2C-P include vivid geometric visuals, extreme time dilation, deep introspection, and intense emotional shifts. At moderate doses, users report enhanced sensory perception, euphoria, and philosophical or existential thinking. At high doses, it can induce profound ego dissolution, synesthesia, and overwhelming hallucinations, sometimes leading to paranoia, mental loops, or difficulty distinguishing reality from hallucination.

Due to its long duration and high potency, 2C-P is considered a challenging psychedelic, recommended only for experienced users. Its slow onset and prolonged peak make it particularly prone to bad trips if taken in uncontrolled environments or in excessive amounts. Though not as well-known as 2C-B or 2C-E, 2C-P remains one of the most intense and long-lasting substances in the 2C family.

* * *

The New York Subway Identity Crisis, August 1997

JASON A.

Source: NYPD Reports, Medical Evaluations
Location: New York City

A woman took a dangerously high dose of 2C-P before entering the New York subway system and experienced a complete breakdown of her sense of identity. Witnesses reported that she wandered from train to train, stopping frequently to look around with a confused expression. She approached several passengers and asked if they recognized her, insisting that she had forgotten who she was.
As her distress increased, she stopped interacting with people and instead fixated on the subway walls. She stared at the station signs as if they were speaking to her. She began whispering to herself, occasionally nodding as if responding to something only she could hear. Her behavior became more erratic when she pressed her hands against the walls and asked passengers if the words on the signs were trying to help her remember who she was.
A witness recalled that she became increasingly frantic, pacing back and forth and muttering that she was disappearing. She started pulling at her own clothing, saying that she could no longer tell if she was real. Another passenger tried to reassure her, but she ignored them, instead focusing on her reflection in the subway window. She reached out to touch it and gasped, stepping back in fear as if she had just seen a stranger.
Her panic escalated when she suddenly collapsed onto the floor, covering her head and rocking back and forth. She whispered that she was only a collection of memories with no person attached to them. Police were called when she refused to respond to questions, instead repeating that she was a collection of thoughts that no longer belonged to anyone.
When officers arrived, she continued staring at her reflection in the subway window, refusing to acknowledge them. She was eventually restrained and transported to a hospital, where medical staff noted that she remained in a dissociative state for hours. Even after the drug wore off, she expressed confusion

about whether she had ever been a real person or if she had just been an idea that somehow gained awareness.

The Miami Beach Endless Wave Experience, March 2002

Source: Miami-Dade Emergency Medical Reports, Eyewitness Accounts
Location: Miami Beach, Florida

A man took an extremely high dose of 2C-P at Miami Beach and became convinced that he was stuck in an endless wave. Witnesses reported that he ran back and forth along the shoreline, staring at the water with wide eyes and shouting that time had stopped moving.
At first, people assumed he was playing or exercising, but his behavior quickly became more erratic. He kept stopping suddenly, looking at the ocean as if trying to decipher something, then running again. He repeatedly asked people nearby if they could see the waves looping. When no one understood what he meant, he began shaking his head and muttering that he had become part of the pattern and that he would never reach the shore again.
His fear intensified when he waded into the shallow water, repeatedly lifting his arms and dropping them, as if trying to sync himself with the movement of the waves. He whispered that the ocean was breathing and that he was stuck between its inhale and exhale. Several beachgoers attempted to talk to him, but he was unresponsive, staring out at the horizon and saying that he had lost his place in time.
Lifeguards intervened when he suddenly dropped to his knees in the water and refused to move, saying that if he stepped forward, he would sink into infinity. He became distressed when they tried to pull him back to shore, insisting that he had already drowned and that they were just delaying the inevitable.
Paramedics arrived and found him lying on the sand, whispering about repeating moments and endless tides. He was transported to Jackson Memorial Hospital in Miami, where medical staff noted

that he remained in a dissociative state for several hours.

The Las Vegas Casino Infinity Paranoia, July 2010

Source: Las Vegas Metropolitan Police Department, Security Reports
Location: Las Vegas, Nevada

A man took a high dose of 2C-P inside a Las Vegas casino and became convinced that he was trapped in an infinite loop. Witnesses reported that he wandered through the casino floor aimlessly, stopping at different slot machines and staring at them for several minutes before repeating the process.
At first, security staff assumed he was just another intoxicated tourist, but as time passed, his behavior became more unusual. He began muttering to himself, repeating that he had already seen every person in the casino before and that he was stuck in the same moment over and over. When approached by security, he asked them if they were real or if they were part of the loop.
As his paranoia escalated, he became increasingly frantic, stopping random guests and asking if they had just spoken to him before. Some tried to ignore him, while others attempted to reassure him, but he shook his head and backed away each time, insisting that everything was repeating endlessly.
His fear grew when he tried to leave the casino but found himself unable to recognize the exits. He walked toward one doorway, hesitated, turned around, and then tried again, only to stop in confusion. He repeatedly said that every exit led back to the same place. Witnesses recalled that he pressed his hands against the walls and stared at them as if testing whether they were solid.
When security attempted to escort him outside, he resisted, insisting that the casino was not real and that he had to find the right way out before time reset again. His panic reached its peak when he suddenly ran across the floor, shouting that he needed to escape before the cycle repeated.
Police were called when he started trying to climb onto a

roulette table, saying that he needed to see things from a higher perspective to find the real exit. When officers arrived, he was unresponsive to their questions, staring at the lights above him and whispering that they were guiding him to the next version of reality.

He was transported to University Medical Center of Southern Nevada (UMC), where medical staff noted that he remained in a dissociative state for hours. Even after the effects of the drug began to wear off, he continued asking if he had truly escaped or if he was still inside another version of the loop.

The Jersey Shore Infinite Ocean Panic, July 2011

Source: New Jersey State Police, Eyewitness Reports
Location: New Jersey

A man took a dangerously high dose of 2C-P while on the Jersey Shore and became convinced that the ocean was an endless void. Witnesses saw him standing knee-deep in the water, motionless, staring at the horizon as if hypnotized. At first, people thought he was simply admiring the view, but he remained completely still for nearly an hour, barely responding when approached.

When someone asked if he was okay, he muttered that he had stepped off the edge of the Earth and that there was nothing left beyond the waves. His breathing became erratic, and he began stepping backward slowly, as if afraid of falling into something unseen. A couple on the beach overheard him whispering that he was outside of time and that the ocean was swallowing everything.

His paranoia escalated when he suddenly screamed and ran back to shore, falling onto the sand and saying that he had been pulled too far out. He grabbed at the sand with his hands, pressing his body against it as if trying to ground himself. A lifeguard approached and tried to calm him, but he refused to acknowledge them, instead looking up at the sky and repeating that the world had ended and that he was trapped in the afterimage of reality.

JASON A.

Witnesses reported that he started digging in the sand frantically, saying that he had to find the real version of himself before he disappeared completely. When people tried to assist him, he panicked, yelling that they were part of the illusion and that they were only shadows cast by the waves.

Police were called when he ran along the shoreline, screaming that the tide was erasing the world. Officers found him sitting in a fetal position near a dune, rocking back and forth and whispering that he had drifted too far from the center of time. He was unresponsive to their questions and had to be physically restrained when he resisted being moved, insisting that any movement would cause him to dissolve.

He was transported to Jersey Shore University Medical Center in Neptune, New Jersey. He continued expressing fear that he had been permanently disconnected from reality and that the ocean had rewritten history without him.

* * *

Common Themes Across 2C-P Freakouts

Unlike shorter-lasting 2C compounds, 2C-P can last 10 to 20 hours, sometimes even longer at high doses. Its slow onset, sometimes taking up to three hours to fully manifest, has led to accidental overdoses when users mistakenly take more, thinking the first dose was too weak. When a trip turns bad, the combination of prolonged intensity, cognitive overload, and powerful visuals can create deep paranoia and mental exhaustion. Below are some of the most commonly reported themes in 2C-P freakouts.

Time Distortion and the Feeling of Being Stuck

- Many users report that time slows down dramatically, making minutes feel like hours.

- Some become convinced that they are permanently trapped in the psychedelic state and will never return to normal.
- A sense of being caught in a looping experience can create extreme panic and frustration.

Intense Visual Overload and Hallucinatory Fractals

- 2C-P produces powerful geometric hallucinations that can become overwhelming.
- At high doses, users often describe seeing fractals, glowing grids, and endless repeating patterns that seem inescapable.
- Some users lose depth perception, with objects appearing to stretch, melt, or shift unpredictably.

Extreme Paranoia and Perceptual Distortions

- Many users report a growing sense of fear and paranoia, believing they are being watched or followed.
- Some become convinced that they are in an artificial or simulated reality and that the people around them are not real.
- At high doses, 2C-P can cause auditory hallucinations, with users hearing voices, whispers, or incomprehensible sounds.

Cognitive Loops and Thought Overload

- Users often become stuck in repetitive thought loops, feeling unable to break free from a single idea or fear.
- The mind may generate excessive, racing thoughts that spiral into confusion and panic.
- Some users report existential dread, questioning the nature of existence and struggling with thoughts of being permanently altered.

Physical Stimulation and Uncontrollable Restlessness

- 2C-P has stimulating effects that can make it difficult to sit still or

relax.
- Some users feel internal pressure or energy surges that cause excessive pacing, shaking, or tension.
- At very high doses, overstimulation can lead to sweating, nausea, muscle tightness, or an uncomfortable body load.

Dissociation and Ego Fragmentation

- Some individuals experience a complete breakdown of their sense of self, losing their identity or merging with their surroundings.
- At peak intensity, users may feel as though they no longer exist or that they have become part of an infinite reality.
- Feelings of depersonalization and detachment can persist for hours, making the experience disorienting and unsettling.

Resistance to Help and Intervention

- Many users in the middle of a 2C-P freakout refuse assistance, fearing that seeking help will trap them in their altered state permanently.
- Some may resist medical intervention, believing that paramedics or police are part of a larger conspiracy.
- Others become unresponsive, withdrawing completely from their surroundings and entering a state of catatonic dissociation.

Final Thoughts:

2C-P freakouts can be among the most mentally and physically exhausting psychedelic experiences, due to the combination of extreme duration, intense visuals, cognitive loops, and overwhelming paranoia. Unlike shorter-lasting psychedelics like 2C-B or LSD, 2C-P offers no quick relief once a trip turns bad, leaving users mentally drained and physically tense for hours on end. The delayed onset and long-lasting effects make it particularly dangerous for overdosing, leading to experiences that can feel impossible to escape.

DPT

Having witnessed the sometimes terrifying effects of DOM and other phenethylamines, amphetamine based psychedelic, we now move on to some tryptamine bad trip reports. Unlike DOx compounds, DPT, or N,N-Dipropyltryptamine, is a psychedelic tryptamine first synthesized in the 1950s by American chemists exploring variations of naturally occurring compounds like DMT. It was initially investigated for its potential use in psychotherapy and religious experiences due to its intense hallucinogenic effects. The effects of DPT are typically long-lasting, with a duration of around 2 to 6 hours when smoked or injected, and up to 8 to 12 hours when taken orally with an MAOI. Its onset is rapid when smoked but slower when taken orally. The experience is known for being highly immersive, with users reporting intense visual distortions, a sense of ego dissolution, and powerful emotional or spiritual insights. Unlike DMT, which is often described as dreamlike and otherworldly, DPT tends to produce a more overwhelming and sometimes chaotic experience, with unpredictable shifts in perception and reality. High doses can lead to extreme dissociation, auditory hallucinations, and a strong sense of encountering otherworldly entities or religious experiences.

❋ ❋ ❋

The Berkeley Marina Ocean Dissolution, July 1988

Source: Berkeley Police Logs, Coast Guard Reports
Location: Berkeley, California

A woman took an extremely high dose of DPT near the Berkeley Marina and gradually became convinced that she was merging with the ocean. Witnesses reported that she stood ankle-deep in the water for over an hour, completely still, whispering to herself that she was no longer a person but a wave in the sea. She repeatedly looked down at her hands and arms, moving them slowly through the air as if testing whether they were still attached to her body.

Her behavior became more concerning when she began wading deeper into the water, murmuring that she could feel herself dissolving. When a passerby asked if she needed help, she turned and smiled at them but spoke in a quiet, detached voice, saying that she had already let go and that there was nothing left to save. She continued moving further into the bay, ignoring people calling out to her.

Her distress escalated when she suddenly threw her arms into the air and shouted that she had lost her body completely. Witnesses described her expression as both ecstatic and terrified, as though she were caught between awe and panic. She started spinning in circles, splashing water around herself, and repeatedly asking where the shoreline had gone.

Coast Guard officers were alerted by a nearby boat and arrived as she was swimming farther out, insisting that she could not come back because she no longer belonged to the land. When officers attempted to intervene, she resisted, screaming that returning to shore would mean losing her connection to eternity. She briefly submerged herself underwater, causing further panic among the responders.

After being pulled from the water, she remained unresponsive to questioning, staring at the waves with wide eyes. She was transported to Alta Bates Medical Center, where medical staff noted that she was in a highly agitated state and required sedation.

The Ashby BART Station Time Displacement Incident, November 1989

Source: BART Security Reports, Medical Evaluations

JASON A.

Location: Berkeley, California

A man took a high dose of DPT while waiting at Ashby BART Station and experienced a severe breakdown in his perception of time. Witnesses reported that he was standing near the platform, checking his watch repeatedly, shaking his head, and muttering that the train was never coming because time had stopped moving. His confusion grew more intense as he started looking at the people around him, asking if they were real or if they had been frozen in place with him.
As minutes passed, he sat down on a bench and buried his head in his hands, whispering that every second was repeating infinitely. A woman who attempted to check on him said he looked at her in terror and asked how long she had been there, insisting that he had seen her walk past him over and over again. His paranoia escalated when he got up suddenly and began pacing along the platform, staring at the train schedule as if trying to break free from a loop.
His distress reached a peak when a train arrived, and he refused to board, claiming that stepping onto it would cause him to be erased from time entirely. BART security officers approached him, but he ignored them, continuing to stare at his surroundings as if analyzing whether anything had changed. When they asked him for identification, he responded by saying he had forgotten how long he had been alive and that every version of himself was overlapping.
When the train left, he sat back down, rocking slightly, and telling the officers that he had missed his chance to return to reality. He covered his ears and refused to answer questions, insisting that if he spoke, he might reset everything again. At this point, security detained him and called for medical assistance.
He was transported to Alta Bates Medical Center, where medical staff reported that he remained in a dissociative state for several hours.

✳ ✳ ✳

Common Themes Across DPT Freakouts

DPT is known for its intense dissociative and hallucinogenic effects. Unlike other psychedelics, DPT is often described as deeply immersive, chaotic, and unpredictable, with users reporting overwhelming visual distortions, ego dissolution, and a sense of being thrown into another reality. Depending on the method of ingestion, effects can last 2 to 6 hours when smoked or injected and up to 8 to 12 hours when taken orally with an MAOI. At high doses, DPT is notorious for creating extreme states of fear, paranoia, and a total loss of self-awareness, making freakouts particularly intense and difficult to manage. Below are some of the most commonly reported themes in DPT freakouts.

Time Distortion and Perception of Infinity

- Many users experience a complete breakdown of time, feeling as though they are trapped in an endless moment.
- Some become convinced that time has stopped or that they have permanently left linear reality.
- The sensation of existing outside of time can lead to extreme confusion and panic.

Overwhelming Visual and Auditory Hallucinations

- DPT produces intense and often terrifying visual hallucinations, including shifting dimensions, tunnels, and flashing patterns.
- Users frequently report hearing otherworldly voices, chants, or mechanical buzzing sounds.
- Some users feel as though they are dissolving into a chaotic, pulsating void with no connection to the physical world.

Ego Dissolution and Identity Loss

- Many users describe DPT as stripping away their sense of self, leading to a terrifying feeling of complete ego death.

- Some become convinced that they have died or are experiencing the afterlife.
- The loss of personal identity can make it difficult to distinguish between internal thoughts and external reality.

Religious or Mystical Delusions

- High-dose DPT experiences often include visions of deities, spirits, or abstract entities.
- Some users report feeling like they are being judged, tested, or initiated into a higher order of consciousness.
- Others believe they have merged with the universe, lost their individuality, or been given divine knowledge that they can no longer comprehend once the trip fades.

Paranoia and Fear of Being Trapped
- Many users feel as though they have been kidnapped by an unknown force or are stuck in an alternate dimension.
- Some report feelings of being observed by powerful, unseen entities.
- The overwhelming nature of the experience can make users believe they will never return to normal, leading to extreme distress.

Physical Sensations and Loss of Control

- Users frequently report intense body vibrations, feelings of disintegration, or the sensation of being pulled apart.
- Some describe floating out of their body or feeling paralyzed while their mind travels elsewhere.
- The combination of mental and physical intensity can lead to nausea, trembling, or uncontrollable movements.

Resistance to Help and Confusion About Reality

- Many users in the middle of a DPT freakout refuse assistance,

believing that those trying to help are part of their hallucination.
- Some may act unpredictably, lash out, or enter a catatonic state, making intervention difficult.
- Others completely withdraw from their surroundings, refusing to communicate until the effects wear off.

Final Thoughts:

DPT freakouts can be among the most intense and psychologically overwhelming psychedelic experiences, often characterized by total ego dissolution, extreme hallucinations, and a complete loss of connection to reality. Its rapid onset and deeply immersive nature make it especially difficult for users to control their experience once it turns negative. Unlike more forgiving psychedelics like LSD or psilocybin, DPT provides little room for comfort or grounding, making bad trips especially terrifying and exhausting.

LSD

LSD hardly needs an introduction, as it is one of the most well-known psychedelics in history. First synthesized in 1938 by Albert Hofmann, LSD, or lysergic acid diethylamide, is a potent tryptamine hallucinogen that profoundly alters perception, thought, and consciousness. Its effects can last between 8 and 12 hours, producing vivid visual distortions, time dilation, intense introspection, and occasionally, overwhelming existential experiences. While some users report deep spiritual insights and euphoria, others experience paranoia, looping thoughts, or a complete loss of self-identity, especially at high doses. Its role in counterculture movements, scientific research, and personal exploration has made LSD both infamous and fascinating. While those who experienced terrifying LSD trips often endured profound fear and confusion, they at least had the benefit of a shorter duration, unlike phenethylamines like DOM. Bad DOx trips often seemed to stretch endlessly, still growing in intensity even up to eight hours later according to some reports, leaving users trapped in an escalating nightmare with no clear end in sight.

Unlike in the case of DOM, Thorazine and other sedatives are actually quite helpful in alleviating some of the more severe effects of a bad LSD trip, rather than worsening them. Thorazine, an antipsychotic, works by blocking dopamine receptors and dampening sensory overload, helping to bring users back to a calmer, more grounded state. Meanwhile, benzodiazepines like Valium or Librium enhance GABA, the brain's primary inhibitory neurotransmitter, reducing panic and agitation. These medications help shorten the duration and intensity of a bad trip, relieve paranoia and delusions, and allow the user to relax rather than spiral further into distress.

* * *

The Berkeley Campus Glass Shattering Illusion, March 1966

Source: UC Berkeley Campus Security, Hospital Reports
Location: Berkeley, California

A student took an extremely high dose of LSD on campus and became convinced that the walls and windows of every building were made of fragile glass. Witnesses reported that he walked cautiously, stepping as if the ground might break beneath him. He repeatedly warned people around him to be careful, insisting that reality itself was on the verge of shattering. As his paranoia grew, he began inspecting the surfaces of walls and doors, running his hands over them and whispering that he could feel the cracks forming.

His distress escalated when he suddenly stopped in the middle of the courtyard and stared at the sky, claiming that he could see fissures forming in the air. He started yelling at students to stay back, warning them that if they touched anything, the entire world might collapse. A professor passing by tried to calm him, but he ignored their words, insisting that he was the only one who could see the truth.

Moments later, he sprinted toward a brick wall and threw himself against it, screaming that he needed to break through to reach the real world. The impact knocked him to the ground, but he immediately got up and tried again, convinced that the barrier was just an illusion. Onlookers restrained him before he could injure himself further, though he continued to struggle and shout that the universe was made of brittle glass and that he was already breaking apart.

Campus security arrived and attempted to talk him down, but he remained in a state of extreme agitation. He refused to sit still, pacing in tight circles and waving his hands in front of his face as if trying to catch fragments of reality before they disappeared. When paramedics arrived, he resisted being taken to the hospital, crying that the ambulance was just another layer of the illusion. Medical staff noted that he remained in a highly dissociated state for hours, occasionally reaching out and running his fingers along the walls of his hospital room as if checking for cracks. Even after the drug had worn off, he continued expressing fear that reality was unstable and that the walls around him could collapse at any moment.

The People's Park Cosmic Spiral Collapse, May 1967

Source: Berkeley Barb, Medical Reports
Location: Berkeley, California

In May 1967, a man took LSD at People's Park, expecting a profound and expansive experience. As the effects deepened, he became convinced that he was spiraling into the universe. Witnesses reported that he stood motionless for hours, staring at the sky and whispering about galaxies forming inside his mind. He spoke in fragmented phrases, describing how his thoughts were expanding outward like cosmic waves. When people attempted to communicate with him, he did not respond at first, as if he had lost connection to normal reality. Eventually, when someone touched his shoulder, he screamed that his body had dissolved into stardust and that he was no longer part of the physical world.

As the experience intensified, he dropped to his knees and began running his hands through the dirt, claiming that he was merging with the planet. At one point, he lay down on the grass, stretched out his arms, and whispered that he had become the entire cosmos. Those around him became concerned when he stopped reacting to external stimuli and remained in a catatonic state.

Hours later, paramedics arrived to find him still lying in the grass, his breathing shallow and his eyes unfocused. When they attempted to lift him, he mumbled that he had already ascended beyond physical form and could not return. He was transported to a hospital, where medical staff reported that he remained nonverbal for several more hours. Even after the drug had begun to wear off, he expressed lingering dissociation and confusion, questioning whether he had truly come back from the cosmic spiral or if he was still lost in it.

This case became one of the more extreme high-dose LSD freakouts in Berkeley, illustrating how the drug's effects could lead to overwhelming dissociation, a complete detachment from reality, and an intense belief in personal transformation beyond the physical self.

The Telegraph Avenue Infinite Mirror Crisis Date, October 1968

Source: Eyewitness Accounts, Berkeley Police Logs
Location: Berkeley, California

In October 1968, a woman took a high dose of LSD while on Telegraph Avenue. As the effects intensified, she became completely fixated on her reflection in a store window. Witnesses reported that she stood motionless for hours, staring into the glass as if she were in conversation with someone. She began speaking softly to her reflection, asking why they were separate and why she felt like she was looking at another version of herself in a different world.

As time passed, her fixation turned into panic. She started pressing her hands against the glass, saying that she could feel herself splitting into multiple versions. Her breathing became rapid, and she backed away suddenly, screaming that she was fracturing into infinite realities and would never return to being whole. She ran up and down the street, stopping at different reflective surfaces and looking into them with desperation, as if searching for an answer.

At one point, she sat on the sidewalk, gripping her head and muttering that she had become lost between dimensions. Police were called when she began shouting at her reflection, accusing it of keeping her trapped in an illusion. When officers arrived, she was unresponsive to questions, instead whispering to herself about needing to find the real version of her body before it was too late.

She was eventually taken to a hospital, where medical staff noted that she remained in a state of extreme confusion for several hours. Even after the drug wore off, she expressed lingering paranoia that she was still split between multiple versions of herself and could not determine which one was real.

This case became one of the more unsettling high-dose LSD freakouts in Berkeley, highlighting the drug's ability to induce profound identity distortions and the terrifying belief that reality itself had shattered into infinite reflections.

The Prudential Tower High-Rise Panic, August 1969

Source: Boston Emergency Medical Services, Eyewitness Accounts
Location: Boston, Massachusetts

A man took LSD and visited the Prudential Tower, where he became increasingly overwhelmed by the height and the altered perception of space caused by the psychedelic. As the effects intensified, he became convinced that he was no longer physically connected to the ground and that he was floating above the city. Witnesses on the observation deck reported that he initially stood still for several minutes, staring out at the skyline in a trance-like state before abruptly clutching the railing and screaming that gravity had stopped working.

His panic escalated when he began claiming that the buildings below him were shifting positions and that the city itself was unraveling. He repeatedly asked other visitors whether they could still see the ground or if they had, like him, become untethered from reality. When no one confirmed his delusion, he grew more agitated, pacing along the railing and insisting that he had to find a way to reattach himself to the physical world.

At one point, he attempted to climb over the railing, believing that if he stepped into the sky, he would either regain control of his body or fully dissolve into the atmosphere. Security officers intervened just in time, physically restraining him as he fought to break free, shouting that he was being pulled into another dimension.

Emergency medical responders arrived and sedated him before transporting him to a nearby hospital, where he remained in a dissociative state for several hours. Medical staff reported that he continued expressing fear that he was still floating above the earth long after the LSD had begun to wear off. Though he eventually regained his composure, he later admitted that the experience left him with a lingering sense of detachment from reality, struggling to fully trust his perception of gravity and space for weeks after the incident.

The Telegraph Avenue Infinite Hallway Incident, September 1969

Source: Berkeley Police Logs, Eyewitness Reports
Location: Berkeley, California

A man took a dangerously high dose of LSD while on Telegraph Avenue and began experiencing extreme spatial distortions. Witnesses reported that he started looking down the street with a dazed expression, muttering that the road was stretching endlessly in both directions. At first, he seemed fascinated by the sensation, but within minutes, his fascination turned into panic. He began asking strangers if they could see the walls closing in and insisted that he was trapped in an infinite hallway.

As his paranoia grew, he started walking in one direction, then abruptly stopping, looking around in confusion before turning back. He did this repeatedly, as if he were testing whether the street had an exit. When people tried to reassure him that he could leave whenever he wanted, he shook his head and said that there were no doors, only more of the same hallway repeating forever.

He then started knocking on invisible doors in the air, claiming that there had to be a way out. When none of them opened, he became visibly distressed, accusing pedestrians of being part of the illusion and preventing him from leaving. His frustration escalated when he tried to run but suddenly stopped, staring at the ground and whispering that he had just passed the same spot for the thousandth time.

Police arrived after multiple reports of a man shouting and acting erratically in the street. When officers approached, he backed away, demanding to know if they were real or if they were just echoes of himself. He continued pacing in circles, mumbling about needing to find the right door before it disappeared.

He was eventually restrained and taken to a hospital, where medical staff noted that he remained in a highly paranoid state for several hours. Even after the drug wore off, he expressed lingering fears that he was still trapped in an endless hallway and that his entire life had been looping without him realizing it.

The Berkeley Campus Reality Fracture, April 1970

Source: UC Berkeley Campus Security, Medical Records
Location: Berkeley, California

In April 1970, a student took an overwhelming dose of LSD While on campus. As the effects deepened, he began experiencing extreme distortions of time and space, becoming convinced that reality itself was breaking apart. Witnesses reported that he initially appeared dazed, standing in the middle of the crowd with a blank expression, his eyes darting around as if he were seeing something others could not. He began murmuring that time was looping, that the same moment was happening over and over again.

He turned to different people and asked if they were real, claiming that everything felt like an illusion. His voice became frantic as he repeated that he was witnessing the same second repeat endlessly and that he had fallen outside of time. When people tried to reassure him, he backed away, shaking his head and saying that

they were only echoes of something that had already happened.
His behavior became more erratic when he suddenly sat down on the pavement and held his head in his hands, rocking back and forth and whispering that he was dissolving into nothing. At one point, he started clawing at the ground as if trying to hold onto reality, telling those around him that he could feel himself fading. When campus security arrived, he did not respond to their questions, instead repeating that he had already said everything before and that there was no way to escape the repeating moment. He was taken to a hospital, where medical staff observed that he remained dissociated for hours, still convinced that time was looping and that he had never actually existed. Even after the effects of the drug wore off, he struggled with lingering confusion and a deep fear that reality was unstable.

The Tilden Park Dissolution Freakout, July 1972

Source: Park Ranger Reports, Emergency Room Records
Location: Berkeley, California

In July 1972, a group of hikers took LSD while exploring Tilden Park together. As the effects intensified, several members of the group began experiencing severe dissociation and an overwhelming sense of detachment from reality. Witnesses reported that one individual suddenly stopped walking and stared at the trees, whispering that he could feel himself merging with them. He refused to move, insisting that he had become part of the forest and that walking away would tear him apart.
Another member of the group became convinced that he had lost his physical form entirely. He wandered off the trail, touching his arms and legs repeatedly while muttering that he was turning into pure energy. At one point, he attempted to walk through solid objects, believing that his body had dissolved into light and could pass through matter. When his friends tried to stop him, he became confused and accused them of trying to keep him from ascending to another plane of existence.

The situation worsened when a third hiker collapsed onto the ground, staring at the sky and whispering that he was floating away. He repeatedly asked if the ground was still real and if gravity was holding him in place. Another hiker became so overwhelmed by visual distortions that he covered his eyes and refused to open them, claiming that the entire world was melting and that he was afraid he would disappear if he looked at anything.

Concerned park visitors contacted rangers after finding members of the group wandering aimlessly, some in a state of complete confusion and others visibly distressed. When rangers arrived, they found one individual hugging a tree and refusing to let go, another lying on the ground in a catatonic state, and a third repeatedly asking if he was still alive. Several members of the group were unable to answer basic questions about where they were or what was happening.

The group was transported to a hospital, where medical staff noted that they remained in a highly dissociated state for several hours. Even after the effects of the drug had worn off, some of them continued experiencing lingering visual distortions and difficulty distinguishing between hallucination and reality.

The Santa Monica Pier Ocean Infinity Crisis, June 1982

Source: LAPD Reports, Emergency Room Records
Location: Los Angeles, California

Description: A man took LSD while at the Santa Monica Pier, expecting a heightened sense of awareness and deep connection to the ocean. As the drug's effects intensified, witnesses noticed him staring at the waves for an extended period, completely still. He eventually began whispering to himself, shaking his head as if struggling to understand something.

Suddenly, he took off running down the beach, his arms outstretched, shouting that the ocean had no end and that he was being pulled into infinity. People nearby tried to calm him, but he was unresponsive, his eyes darting back and forth as he repeatedly turned to look at the horizon. When a bystander attempted to stop him from running too close to the water, he pulled away and accused them of being part of the illusion that was keeping him trapped.

His paranoia escalated when he fell to his knees, digging his hands into the wet sand and screaming that he was disappearing. He told those around him that he could feel himself stretching across time, that the waves were swallowing his existence, and that he would never be able to find where he had started.

Police arrived after multiple reports of a man behaving erratically on the beach. When officers approached, he ran toward the water, insisting that he had already begun dissolving and that there was no reason to resist. Officers managed to stop him before he entered deeper water, but he continued struggling and screaming that the ocean had absorbed him and that nothing was real anymore.

He was eventually taken to Santa Monica Hospital, now part of UCLA Santa Monica Medical Center, where medical staff reported that he remained dissociated for several hours, unable to recognize his own reflection. Even after the drug's effects wore off, he expressed lingering fears that he had been lost somewhere in the horizon and that the world around him was just a fragment of what remained.

The Lake Merritt Time Fracture Incident, September 1983

Source: Eyewitness Reports, Medical Evaluations
Location: Oakland, California

A woman took LSD while at Lake Merritt and quickly became overwhelmed by severe temporal distortions. Witnesses reported that she stood motionless at the lake's edge for an extended period, staring at the water as if frozen in time. She was whispering to herself, repeating that something was wrong. When a passerby asked if she was okay, she turned to them with wide eyes and asked if time was still moving.

As minutes passed, she began to cry, saying that she had been stuck in the same second for an eternity. She grabbed at her clothes and looked at her hands, as if checking to see if she had changed. One witness recalled that she was frantically looking at her watch and shaking her head, muttering that the numbers didn't make sense. At one point, she dropped to the ground and began tracing numbers in the dirt, insisting that she had to reassemble time before it was too late.

Her paranoia escalated when people tried to reassure her. She told them that they were only echoes of a moment that had already happened, that none of them were real. As she became more distressed, she covered her ears and curled into a ball, saying that she could hear time splitting apart around her.

Police were called when she refused to move or speak coherently. When officers arrived, she stared at them in confusion, as if trying to determine if they existed. She was taken to Highland Hospital, where she repeatedly asked what day and time it was, convinced that she had been looping in the same instant forever.

Medical staff later reported that she remained in a highly dissociated state for several hours, unable to tell whether she was awake or still trapped in the loop. Even after the drug had worn off, she continued to express fear that time was still broken and that she might never truly escape the moment she had been stuck in.

The Telegraph Avenue Melting Faces Incident, September 1983

Source: Berkeley Police Reports, Eyewitness Statements
Location: Berkeley, California

A woman took a high dose of LSD while walking on Telegraph Avenue and began experiencing extreme visual distortions. Witnesses reported that she suddenly stopped in the middle of the sidewalk, staring at the people around her with wide eyes. She whispered that their faces were melting, stretching and dripping like wax. Her breathing became erratic as she backed away, looking from person to person, as if trying to confirm what she was seeing.

She approached several strangers, touching their faces lightly before recoiling in horror. She then grabbed her own face and started rubbing it frantically, gasping that she could not remember what she looked like. Her distress increased as she turned to a store window and stared at her reflection, her mouth slightly open as if she had seen something unrecognizable. She pressed her hands against the glass, whispering that her face was also melting, and that soon there would be nothing left of her.

As her panic escalated, she began crying and shaking her head, insisting that she was disappearing. She ran a short distance, stopping again to check her reflection in another window, only to break down in fresh terror. Several bystanders attempted to calm her, but she became unresponsive to their words, fixated on her own distorted image.

Police arrived after receiving reports of a woman in distress, unable to move from the sidewalk. When officers approached her, she did not react, continuing to stare into the glass, whispering that she had already melted away. She was eventually taken to a hospital, where medical staff noted that she remained dissociated for hours. Even after the drug wore off, she expressed lingering fear that her face had permanently changed and that she could no longer recognize herself.

The Oakland Tribune Building Dissolution Crisis, March 1986

Source: Oakland Police Reports, Emergency Room Records
Location: Oakland, California

A man took an unknown dose of LSD near the Oakland Tribune Building and quickly became overwhelmed by intense visual distortions. Witnesses reported that he started staring at the building with an expression of fear, pointing at it and mumbling that it was melting. At first, people thought he was joking, but as time passed, he became more agitated, pacing in circles and insisting that the entire structure was dissolving into liquid.

His panic escalated when he fell to the ground, clutching the pavement and begging people to help him before everything disappeared. He shouted that reality itself was breaking apart and that if no one stopped it, the entire city would dissolve. A bystander tried to reassure him, but he refused to listen, repeatedly rubbing his hands against the sidewalk as if trying to anchor himself in place.

As his paranoia grew, he began crawling away from the building, saying that he could feel the ground vanishing beneath him. Several people attempted to calm him, but he screamed that they were part of the illusion and that they were disappearing too. His behavior became so erratic that multiple witnesses called the police.

When officers arrived, he initially refused to acknowledge them, staring past them and whispering about the city turning into liquid. He resisted being moved, insisting that any movement would cause him to dissolve as well. Eventually, police managed to restrain him and transport him to Highland Hospital, which was the primary facility handling psychiatric emergencies and drug-related crises in the area at the time. Medical staff reported that he remained highly disoriented for several hours. Even after the effects of the LSD began to wear off, he continued expressing uncertainty about whether the world around him was real or still dissolving.

The Vista Hermosa Park Sky Melting Panic, August 1987

Source: LAPD Dispatch Logs, Emergency Room Records
Location: Los Angeles, California

A man took LSD in Vista Hermosa Park and quickly became overwhelmed by intense visual hallucinations. Witnesses reported that he was staring up at the sky with wide eyes, barely blinking, as if he were watching something others could not see. He began muttering under his breath that the clouds were dripping, saying that the sky itself was melting.

As time passed, his breathing became irregular, and he started backing away from open spaces, pressing himself against trees and benches as if seeking shelter. He repeatedly whispered that the air was turning into liquid and that soon, everything would be submerged. His distress escalated when he turned toward downtown Los Angeles and gasped, pointing at the buildings in the distance, insisting that they were also dissolving.

He ran toward several strangers, grabbing their arms and pleading with them to tell him if they were melting too. Some attempted to calm him, but he became more erratic, shouting that everything was turning into a fluid state and that he had to escape before he dissolved completely. When someone tried to guide him to sit down, he pulled away, screaming that touching anything would cause him to lose his form.

Paramedics were called after he collapsed near a walking path, clutching his head and whispering that he was already gone. When emergency responders arrived, he refused to acknowledge them at first, staring at the sky with a blank expression. He eventually agreed to be transported to a hospital but continued murmuring that reality had turned into water and that he could no longer tell if he was solid or not. He was taken to Los Angeles County+USC Medical Center. This hospital was a primary facility for handling psychiatric emergencies and drug-related crises in Los Angeles at the time.

Medical staff reported that he remained in a deeply dissociated state for several hours. Even after the LSD began to wear off, he continued expressing fear that he had permanently lost his physical form and that at any moment, he might dissolve into nothing.

❊ ❊ ❊

Common Themes Across LSD Freakouts

LSD is one of the most well-known and widely used psychedelics, with effects lasting between 8 and 14 hours. While LSD is often associated with positive, life-changing experiences, it can also lead to overwhelming and terrifying bad trips, particularly at high doses or in uncontrolled settings. The combination of intense visuals, altered thought patterns, and heightened emotions can create extreme anxiety, paranoia, and a sense of losing touch with reality. Below are some of the most commonly reported themes in LSD freakouts.

Time Distortion and the Feeling of Being Trapped

- Many users experience extreme time dilation, where minutes feel like hours or even days.
- Some become convinced that the trip will never end and that they are permanently stuck in an altered state.
- Checking clocks or trying to measure time often increases panic and confusion.

Overwhelming Visual and Perceptual Distortions

- LSD produces intense geometric patterns, color shifts, and movement in static objects.
- At high doses, users often see their environment morph, melt, or fragment, making reality feel unstable.
- Some experience double vision, trails, or "breathing walls," which can become overwhelming and induce fear.

Extreme Paranoia and Delusions of Persecution

- Some users develop a sense that they are being watched, followed, or controlled by an unknown force.
- Paranoia can manifest as believing that friends, family, or strangers are conspiring against them.
- In extreme cases, users become convinced they are in a simulation, an experiment, or an alternate reality.

Thought Loops and Cognitive Overload

- LSD can cause racing thoughts and repetitive mental loops, trapping users in obsessive thinking patterns.
- Some individuals struggle with existential questions, feeling overwhelmed by thoughts of life, death, and reality.
- Cognitive overload can make it difficult to focus or communicate, leading to frustration and panic.

Loss of Identity and Ego Dissolution

- High doses of LSD can cause users to lose their sense of self, leading to confusion about their identity.
- Some experience complete ego dissolution, feeling as though they no longer exist as an individual.
- This loss of self can be deeply disorienting and, in a negative mindset, can feel like death or insanity.

Sensory Overload and Physical Discomfort

- LSD heightens sensory perception, sometimes leading to overwhelming sound, light, or tactile sensations.
- Some users feel a sense of physical discomfort, nausea, or tension in the body that adds to anxiety.
- High doses can cause a feeling of being stretched, pulled, or physically melting, which can be distressing.

Resistance to Help and Confusion About Reality

- Many individuals experiencing an LSD freakout resist help, fearing that accepting assistance will make things worse.
- Some become agitated or combative, believing they need to escape or hide from those around them.
- Others withdraw completely, becoming unresponsive and detached from their surroundings.

JASON A.

Final Thoughts:

LSD freakouts can be some of the most intense and distressing psychedelic experiences due to the combination of time distortion, paranoia, thought loops, and identity loss. Unlike shorter-acting psychedelics, LSD's long duration makes it difficult to escape a bad trip once it starts, leading to prolonged anxiety and mental exhaustion. For those who take extremely high doses, the experience can feel completely overwhelming, with a sense of permanent separation from reality. While many people have positive experiences with LSD, those who encounter a bad trip often describe it as one of the most terrifying and mentally exhausting experiences of their lives.

PCP

And now we transition from the sometimes terrifying and overwhelming effects of the phenethylamines and tryptamines and venture into the truly macabre and deeply unsettling realm of PCP. Here, bad trips don't just disorient but often spiral into violent delirium, psychosis, and horrifying dissociation—far removed from the cosmic dread of LSD or DOx, these experiences teeter on the edge of complete psychological and physical ruin—sometimes slipping over entirely.

PCP, or phencyclidine, was first synthesized in 1926 by the pharmaceutical company Parke-Davis as a potential intravenous anesthetic. Initially used in medical settings, it was later discontinued for human use in the 1960s due to severe psychiatric side effects, including hallucinations, paranoia, and dissociation. During this time, researchers studying PCP noticed its profound mind-altering effects, and samples began circulating in underground psychedelic communities. By the late 1960s, illicit labs began producing PCP for recreational use, capitalizing on its dissociative and hallucinogenic properties. The drug was often marketed as a cheaper alternative to LSD, but users quickly discovered its unpredictable and sometimes violent side effects, leading to a notorious reputation.

By the early 1970s, PCP had become a widespread street drug, particularly in cities like Los Angeles, San Francisco, and New York. It was commonly sold as a powder, pill, or liquid, with users often smoking it on cigarettes or marijuana joints ("dipping" or "getting wet"). The drug became associated with erratic behavior, violent outbursts, and dissociative blackouts, earning street names like angel dust, embalming fluid, and rocket fuel.

Mild Dose (1–5 mg)

Users often describe a sensation of profound detachment—feeling emotionally and physically numb, as if separated from their body or surroundings. They may move with slurred speech, unsteady gait, or appear frozen in a blank stare, sometimes accompanied by involuntary eye movements or a catatonic posture. Despite this disconnection, some users report paradoxical feelings of strength or invulnerability. Physiologically, mild doses may trigger elevated heart rate, increased blood pressure, shallow breathing, and a sense of sedation or sluggishness.

Medium Dose (5–10 mg)

At moderate doses, users often describe deeper dissociation: heightened analgesia, a calming sense of detachment, and alterations in sensory perception. Speech becomes more slurred, coordination further impaired, and cognitive processing noticeably slowed. Hallucinations may emerge—shifts in visual and auditory perception that feel vivid yet disconcerting. Many report a marked sense of disconnection from reality, where familiar environments feel strange or dreamlike.

High Dose (>10 mg and beyond)

High doses typically provoke intense and often overwhelming effects. Users often report full-blown hallucinations, psychotic episodes, acute paranoia, and a complete breakdown of ego boundaries. Feelings of omnipotence or invulnerability may escalate into delusions of invincibility, yet are frequently accompanied by confusion, aggression, panic, or violent outbursts. In extreme cases, users describe convulsions, catatonia, or slipping into a coma-like state. Physically, high doses can induce severe hypertension, rapid breathing, hyperthermia, irregular heartbeat, and even life-threatening symptoms including seizures and renal failure.

❆ ❆ ❆

PCP User Believes He Is the Devil, Tries to Eat His Own Hand, August 22, 1974

Source: Chicago Tribune
Location: Chicago, Illinois

A Chicago man was arrested after being found chewing on his own hand, convinced he was the Devil and had to "devour himself" to gain power. When officers tried to restrain him, he bit off a piece of his own tongue and spit it at them. He was impervious to tasers and pain, taking multiple baton strikes before finally being subdued. He was taken to Cook County Hospital, where he was kept in restraints for days due to continued violent outbursts.

PCP User Survives Being Shot in the Head and Keeps Fighting, October 3, 1975

Source: Los Angeles Times
Location: Los Angeles, California

A man in Watts, Los Angeles was terrorizing his neighborhood while naked and high on PCP. Police arrived, and he charged at them, shrugging off baton strikes. Officers shot him in the head at close range—but he did not go down. Instead, he grabbed the gun from the officer and continued fighting until he was beaten unconscious.
He was rushed to King/Drew Medical Center, where doctors discovered that the bullet had lodged in his skull but did not fully penetrate his brain. Despite severe head trauma, he remained conscious and combative for hours. He underwent emergency surgery, during which the bullet was successfully removed. He suffered severe skull fractures but miraculously avoided brain damage. After recovery, he was transferred to a psychiatric facility for further evaluation.

JASON A.

Trip on Angel Dust Detoured at Los Angeles Dance, July 9, 1978

Source: Los Angeles Times
Location: Los Angeles, California

Seventeen-year-old "Dave" took PCP (angel dust) before attending a community dance in Los Angeles, with initially euphoric effects. According to media reports, he first felt "powerful, fearless" – shedding his usual shyness and dancing with multiple partners boldly. As the drug wore on, however, Dave's experience turned nightmarish. He became panicked as he felt his consciousness "float" out of his head, and he was gripped by the terrifying belief that he would die if no one held onto him. He hallucinated ghostly hands "trying to drag him" toward an imagined cliff at the edge of the dance floor. Rescued from the bad trip and later hospitalized, Dave's harrowing ordeal on PCP was recounted in the Times as a cautionary tale of a fun night transformed by a drug into a life-threatening panic.

Man on PCP Survives 19 Gunshots and Keeps Fighting, November 18, 1982

Source: Los Angeles Times
Location: Los Angeles, California

A man in South Central Los Angeles was shot 19 times by police while on PCP and kept attacking officers. The incident started when he was seen wandering the street naked, screaming that he was immortal. He punched through a car window, attacking the driver, before police arrived. When police shot him in the chest multiple times, he continued advancing like nothing had happened. After being shot a total of 19 times, he was finally subdued and rushed to Martin Luther King Jr. Community Hospital. Doctors at King/Drew Medical Center performed multiple emergency surgeries to repair internal damage. Several bullets missed vital organs, but he suffered severe damage to muscle tissue and bones. Due to PCP's numbing effects, he showed little to no response to pain even in the hospital. He spent several months recovering but was left with permanent mobility issues. He was later charged with multiple offenses, including assaulting police officers and destruction of property.

PCP-Fueled Rampage: Man on Angel Dust Attacks Police, Runs Through Glass Door, March 15, 1983

Source: San Diego Union-Tribune
Location: San Diego, California

A 29-year-old man high on PCP was reported acting erratically and aggressively in Downtown San Diego. When police arrived, he charged at them with superhuman strength, knocking two officers unconscious. He then ran full speed through a glass sliding door, shattering it completely but not reacting to his injuries. After police tased and beat him with batons, he continued fighting until he was finally restrained.
He was transported to UC San Diego Medical Center, where doctors removed shards of glass from his body. He was later committed to a psychiatric unit after showing continued signs of PCP psychosis.

Naked PCP User Runs Into Fire and Walks Out Unscathed, July 21, 1984

Source: Chicago Tribune
Location: Chicago, Illinois

A man in Chicago smoked PCP and suddenly stripped naked in the middle of a neighborhood street. He then ran directly into a bonfire at a backyard party, standing in the flames for nearly a full minute. Bystanders tried to pull him out, but he fought them off and continued standing in the fire, laughing.
When firefighters arrived, he walked out of the flames as if nothing had happened, with severe third-degree burns but

no reaction to pain. He was taken to Northwestern Memorial Hospital in Chicago, after being subdued by police. At the hospital he continued laughing and speaking gibberish for hours.

PCP User Jumps Off a Bridge, Swims to Shore, and Attacks Rescuers, June 30, 1985

Source: San Francisco Examiner
Location: San Francisco, California

A man in San Francisco, high on PCP, suddenly jumped off the Golden Gate Bridge into the bay. Witnesses were horrified as they saw him hit the water hard—only to swim to shore as if nothing happened. When rescue workers tried to help him, he violently attacked them, biting and clawing at their faces.
It took seven people to restrain him, as he continued screaming that he was "invincible."
He was transported to San Francisco General Hospital for trauma care and psychiatric evaluation. His body sustained multiple fractures, but he continued resisting treatment for hours. He was later transferred to a psychiatric facility for further monitoring.San Francisco General Hospital

PCP User Jumps Off Coronado Bridge and Survives, July 9, 1986

Source: San Diego Evening Tribune
Location: San Diego, California

A man high on PCP jumped off the Coronado Bridge, a 200+ foot drop into San Diego Bay. Witnesses saw him hit the water, float briefly, and then start swimming as if nothing had happened. Harbor Patrol arrived, but he violently resisted rescue attempts, punching and biting officers.
He was taken to Sharp Coronado Hospital, where doctors confirmed multiple broken bones—but he showed no signs of pain. He was later transferred to the psychiatric ward after

continuing to hallucinate and rant about "being chosen by God."

PCP User Walks Into a Bonfire and Stands There Smiling, June 30, 1987

Source: San Diego Reader
Location: San Diego, California

A man at a beach party in Ocean Beach smoked PCP and walked directly into a bonfire. He stood inside the flames for nearly 30 seconds, smiling and not reacting to the pain. Friends tried to pull him out, but he fought them off violently.
He was transported to UC San Diego Burn Center, where he was treated for third-degree burns over 40% of his body. He remained in ICU for weeks but later made a partial recovery.

Woman Feels Like She's Floating on a Magic Carpet, 2003

Source: Erowid
Location: Unknown

"I lay in bed with my eyes closed and started to feel as if I was on a platform that was floating through the sky like on a magic carpet. I started feel like the platform was tilted and I was going to fall of so I opened my eyes and remained still. I still felt like I was on the platform even with my eyes open and had a strange feeling that I really was going to fall off."

Naked Man on PCP Jumps From a Third-Story Window, Keeps Running, May 10, 2011

Source: Los Angeles Times
Location: Los Angeles, California

A man high on PCP in Los Angeles stripped naked, ran through his apartment, and leaped out of a third-story window.

Witnesses reported he landed on concrete, stood up as if nothing happened, and started running.

Police chased him for several blocks, finally tackling him after he attempted to fight bystanders.

He suffered multiple fractures and was taken to Los Angeles County+USC Medical Center but continued to resist arrest at the hospital.

PCP 'Zombie' Attacks Police, Walks Through Taser Shocks, March 29, 2015

Source: Chicago Tribune
Location: Chicago, Illinois

Police responded to a call about a naked man running through traffic in downtown Chicago. When they arrived, the suspect lunged at officers, growling and attempting to bite them. Tasers were ineffective—the man kept advancing even after being shocked multiple times. It took six officers and multiple baton strikes to finally subdue him.

The man was taken to Northwestern Memorial Hospital in Chicago, Illinois after being subdued by police.

* * *

Common Themes Across PCP Freakouts

PCP (Phencyclidine, also known as "Angel Dust") is notorious for causing some of the most extreme, violent, and disturbing drug-related freakouts ever recorded. Unlike LSD or other hallucinogens, PCP does not just distort reality—it completely severs rational thought, increases aggression, and removes pain perception, making users highly dangerous to themselves and others.

Total Pain Resistance and Superhuman Strength

- PCP numbs the body's pain receptors, making users impervious to injuries, tasers, and even gunshots. Many PCP users have continued fighting even with broken bones, deep wounds, or multiple bullet wounds.
- Extreme, Unprovoked Violence

Many PCP users suddenly attack family, friends, or strangers with no warning. Users often believe others are demons, aliens, or government agents trying to harm them.
- Cannibalism and Mutilation

PCP has been linked to multiple cases of flesh-eating behavior, often in psychotic states. Some users chew off their own fingers, lips, or body parts without realizing it.
- Self-Mutilation and Extreme Body Horror

Because PCP blocks pain, some users mutilate themselves without hesitation. Users have cut off body parts, gouged out their own eyes, or chewed off their lips and fingers.

Total Reality Breakdown and Nightmarish Hallucinations

- Users often experience full-immersion hallucinations, sometimes believing they are dead, in hell, or trapped in a loop. Many freakouts involve perceived demonic possession, alien abduction, or government mind control.
- Out-of-Control, Animalistic Behavior

Users often behave like wild animals—growling, snarling, and attacking people randomly. PCP can cause bizarre, robotic movements, sometimes referred to as "robo-walk," or mindless repetition of actions.
- Suicidal or Reckless Behavior and Delusions of Invincibility

PCP users often believe they are immortal and engage in extremely reckless acts. Many have jumped off buildings, walked into fire, or attacked police, thinking they could not be stopped.
- Hyperthermia and Fatal Overheating

PCP can cause dangerously high body temperatures, leading some

users to strip naked and run wildly through the streets. In severe cases, PCP can cause the body to overheat to fatal levels, leading to organ failure.
- Sudden, Unpredictable Mood Swings and Unprovoked Attacks. Users can switch from calm to violent in seconds, making them extremely dangerous and unpredictable. PCP users often do not respond to de-escalation attempts, leading to police using brute force or tasers to stop them.
- Extended Amnesia and Permanent Psychosis
Many PCP users completely forget what happened during their freakout. In extreme cases, the psychosis never fully fades, leaving users permanently paranoid, delusional, or violent.
Final Thoughts:

Final Thoughts:

Unlike most hallucinogens, PCP causes a complete and unpredictable loss of control, often leading to horrific self-harm, violence, and psychotic breaks that last for hours or even days. PCP users often feel no pain—even after severe injuries. Freakouts often involve extreme violence, paranoia, or delusions of invincibility. Users may attack police, resist tasers, and survive gunshot wounds. Self-mutilation is common—people have cut off body parts or eaten their own flesh. Many users suffer long-term psychosis or permanent personality changes.

EPILOGUE

Hypothetically, If You Took DOM (STP), what would you experience? DOM, being a potent psychedelic amphetamine, produces some of the most intense, high-definition, hyper-detailed visuals of any hallucinogen. Unlike LSD, which can sometimes feel dreamy or fluid, DOM often makes reality sharper, more geometric, and overwhelmingly intricate.
Here's how you might perceive colors, patterns, and textures while under the effects of DOM:

1. Colors Become Hyper-Saturated and Electric

Every color looks more vivid, brighter, and glowing, as if reality has been turned to maximum contrast.
Reds, blues, and greens appear "pure"—as if they've been separated into their deepest, most intense forms.
Objects look outlined in neon—a glowing aura surrounds everything, like a surreal cartoon.
Shadows are no longer black, but instead have swirling colors inside them, sometimes shifting between purple, green, and blue.
The sky is not just blue—it shimmers with golden highlights, faint rainbow bands, and a profound sense of depth that seems infinite.

2. Everything Becomes Incredibly Detailed—Too Detailed

The surface of objects has more texture than ever before—wood grain, fabric fibers, or even the skin on your hands appear infinitely detailed, like fractals.
If you stare at a wall, it is not a flat color anymore—instead, it's a

shifting network of microscopic patterns, almost like it's alive.
Looking at a person's face, you might see every individual pore, hair, and even slight changes in skin color that were invisible before.
Text appears hyper-crisp but constantly shifting—if you read a book or sign, the letters might bend, warp, or duplicate themselves.
Small details in objects you never noticed before suddenly "pop"—you may fixate on the intricate weave of a fabric, the microscopic cracks in paint, or the way light refracts through glass.
This extreme level of visual detail, for many, became overwhelming and unwelcome after the eighth or tenth hour, and virtually unbearable beyond.

3. Fractals, Geometric Grids, and Impossible Patterns

If you close your eyes, you might see infinite tunnels made of shifting mandalas, sacred geometry, and rapidly morphing patterns.
Even with open eyes, these fractals may overlay reality, forming on the walls, floor, sky, and even people's faces.
Tiles and brick walls may transform into "breathing" grids, where each brick is a separate moving piece of an impossible puzzle.
The ground seems to ripple and pulse, like a living, shifting liquid of geometric energy.
If you stare at clouds, trees, or natural patterns, they may turn into sacred geometry, Fibonacci spirals, or kaleidoscopic imagery.

4. Light and Shadows Start to Behave Differently

The sun feels unnaturally bright, almost blinding, and casts multi-colored shadows instead of regular darkness.
Streetlights may emit beams of shifting rainbow colors instead of a single hue.
A simple lamp in a room may appear to be pulsing like a star, casting waves of energy instead of normal illumination.

Looking into mirrors or reflective surfaces may create endless, shifting layers of distortion, almost like seeing into parallel realities.
Water surfaces might appear as portals or liquid crystal, reflecting light in ways that seem surreal and impossible.

5. Objects Begin to "Breathe" and Morph

Static objects are no longer static—walls, furniture, and floors subtly expand and contract, like they are "breathing" with an invisible force.
Faces warp and change—you might see someone's expression shift even when they aren't moving.
Your own hands or fingers may appear elongated, distorted, or translucent, almost like they belong to someone else.
Paintings or posters may come to life, with the characters shifting, blinking, or moving inside their frames.
Textures on a wall or carpet may start forming patterns of animals, faces, or symbols that were never there before.

6. Time Feels Like It's Warping Reality

You may see trails or afterimages following every movement, as if reality is slightly delayed.
If you wave your hand, it may appear to leave multiple ghostly copies behind, fading slowly.
You might see every frame of movement broken down into thousands of tiny steps, like an infinite slow-motion replay.
Certain moments feel frozen in time, where you feel like you've been staring at a single scene for an eternity, even though it's only been seconds.
If you stare at a clock, the numbers may dissolve, reverse, or seem to loop endlessly—making it impossible to tell if time is moving forward, backward, or standing still.

7. Auditory Synesthesia (Seeing Sound)

Sounds might produce waves of colors in the air, blending the visual and auditory senses.
Music becomes three-dimensional, with each note forming a separate shape or pulse of light.
Voices seem to echo or stretch, sometimes doubling or tripling into bizarre reverberations.
Silence is never really silent—you may hear a constant buzzing, ringing, or energetic hum in the background.

8. Emotional and Existential Overload

The beauty of colors, textures, and patterns might be so overwhelming that it brings you to tears.
You might feel like you are "seeing reality for the first time", noticing the infinite details that were always there but hidden from normal perception.
Your sense of self may dissolve, making you feel like you are merging with everything around you.
Some moments might feel like the peak of enlightenment, while others might feel like total sensory chaos, impossible to process.

ACKNOWLEDGEMENT

Writing this book has been a deeply immersive journey into the realities of hallucinogenic drug-induced psychosis. This work would not have been possible without extensive research drawn from historical records, news reports, medical case studies, and firsthand accounts of those who have witnessed or experienced these extreme episodes.

I would like to express my gratitude to the following sources, whose documentation and investigative efforts have provided invaluable insight into the disturbing world of psychedelic and dissociative drug freakouts.

Berkeley Free Clinic Volunteers
The New York Times
Haight-Ashbury Free Clinic records
The Berkeley Barb
Berkeley Police
Berkeley Gazette
DEA Diversion Control Division
LA Free Press
Village Voice
Erowid
Venice Beach Police Department
Brooklyn Police Department
MTA
LAPD
Wikipedia
UC Berkeley Campus Security

New York Post
San Diego Union-Tribune
Berkeley Park Rangers
Berkeley Public Library Staff
Los Angeles Times
San Diego Evening Tribune
UC Berkeley Counseling Center
San Francisco Chronicle
San Francisco Police Department
Las Vegas Metropolitan Police Department
New Jersey State Police
BART Police
Oakland Police Department
The National Observer
Chicago Tribune
The New York Times
The Miami Herald
Boston Globe
San Francisco Examiner
San Diego Reader
New York Daily News

Firsthand accounts and eyewitness testimonies:

- Interviews with former users who have survived near-fatal experiences with PCP, DOM, and other hallucinogens

- Testimonies from families of individuals affected by long-term drug-induced psychosis

- Statements from paramedics, firefighters, and emergency responders who have witnessed the unpredictable and violent effects of these substances firsthand

This book is dedicated to the victims, survivors, and families affected by these powerful substances, as well as the medical professionals and law enforcement officers who have worked tirelessly to save lives in the midst of these chaotic and often tragic events.

While the stories contained in this book may be disturbing, they serve as a crucial reminder of the dangers of uncontrolled substance use and the unpredictable nature of these mind-altering drugs. To those who contributed their knowledge, research, and firsthand experiences, thank you. Your insights have made this book possible, and I hope that by sharing these accounts, we can shed light on a dark and often overlooked part of history.

Made in the USA
Monee, IL
27 September 2025